Homer

in

English Criticism

*The Historical Approach
in the Eighteenth Century*

BY

DONALD M. FOERSTER

ARCHON BOOKS

1969

Copyright, 1947, by Yale University Press
Reprinted 1969 with permission of Yale University Press
in an unaltered and unabridged edition

[*Yale Studies in English, Vol. 105*]

SBN: 208 00772 5
Library of Congress Catalog Card Number: 69-15682
Printed in the United States of America

PREFACE

THE latter half of the eighteenth century brought new conceptions of the early poet and poem. Formerly thought of as a great "conscious" artist, Homer was being characterized as an ideal example of the irrational, spontaneous bard of a primitive people. His *Iliad* and *Odyssey*, once regarded as being essentially above time and place, were now being viewed as important sources for information about early literature and society.

A few years ago in investigating the claims of some of Wolf's followers, it seemed to me that there was an evident hiatus in our knowledge of Homeric criticism, that a good deal, at any rate, remained to be said about the gradual development of the historical approach to Homer and the ways in which that approach was used by different authors at different times. It was apparent that no one, including Georg Finsler, author of *Homer in der Neuzeit,* had discussed the contributions of more than three or four British critics of the eighteenth century—at least in sufficient detail. This fact would seem to justify the study which follows, a study beginning with the historical comments on Homer by such writers as Mme. Dacier, Fénelon, Parnell, and Pope, continuing with Blackwell's important *Enquiry* and the Scotch primitivists whom he influenced, and concluding with the English critics, especially Robert Wood, to whom the German critics were heavily indebted. Because the historical interpretation of Homer made its most pronounced advances in England and Scotland during this time, only occasional consideration of the Continental critics would appear to be warranted.

But it is not merely my purpose to cast some light on our modern historical and scientific treatments of this poet. One should remember that a vast new movement in literary theory was under way in England in the early and middle eighteenth century, that literary scholarship was rapidly moving forward, and that Ossian, Chaucer, Shakespeare, and even the poets of Scandinavia and Persia were being reëstimated in accordance with historical standards. To some extent even anticipating the criticism of these poets, the historical approach to Homer is obviously linked with, and a part of, this much larger development and is hence of interest to the student of general literature as well as to the student of the classics. Not only were many of the Homeric critics also critics of the early British poets, and the same methods applied to the study of Homer as to these poets, but direct comparisons were even made between Homer and Ossian,

Virgil, and Tasso, the writers of the Old Testament, of the ballad and the romance. These parallels are important, even as the new approach to Homer is in itself important, because in them are reflected several fundamental aspects of the historical movement: an increasing historical perspective, the doctrines of progress and degeneration, the growing love for scientific fact, the tendency to regard poetry as a means of enabling us to reconstruct the past, and the tendency to associate a particular poem with a particular nation or with a particular period in that nation's history.

To two persons I wish to express my gratitude for the help they gave me when I was preparing this study; namely, Professor Chauncey B. Tinker, under whom I worked at Yale University, and Professor René Wellek of Yale University. In its original form, this book was presented to the Graduate School of Yale University as a dissertation in partial fulfilment of the requirements for the degree of Doctor of Philosophy.

D. M. F.

May, 1946.

CONTENTS

HOMER IN ENGLISH CRITICISM

I

Late Seventeenth Century

"IT is not Homer who is beautiful," Ernest Renan once said, "but Homeric life, the phase in the existence of humanity described by Homer." This statement probably caused little stir when it was made in the year 1852, for the use of poetry to interpret history, like the use of history to interpret poetry, was so general by then that M. Renan was saying nothing that might startle the literary world. In fact, history and art had become so closely linked that it was no longer easy to tell with which a writer was primarily concerned.

To the neoclassicist a hundred and more years earlier Renan's opinion would have seemed shocking and heretical. If he had failed to make an adequate use of history in the study of literature, the formalist at least had not allowed historical matters to crowd out what appeared to him fundamental critical questions. Homeric life might be intriguing. It might be an important subject—to the historian rather than to the critic. A knowledge of Greek customs would certainly heighten one's appreciation of the *Iliad*, but to make these the center of study was to cease being a critic and to start being a sociologist or anthropologist. True, the neoclassicist may not have expressed these opinions in so many words. He had a better idea what should concern the critic than what should not concern him. In following and modifying Aristotle he had no doubt that the critic was above all to regard literature purely as literature and a given poem as a permanent contribution to the pleasure and profit of all mankind. He saw it as his task to consider the *Iliad* not as a poem for and about the Greeks but as a work of value to ancients and moderns alike. He analyzed the unchanging qualities of human nature displayed in it; he spoke of ideal examples of courage, fidelity, and self-sacrifice. He saw in Odysseus the living example of what a man should be, in others of what a man ought not to be. He went on to matters of form—to structure of the plot, to the proper use of supernatural elements and isolated episodes, to the organization of the poem as a whole. He tried to discover how contemporary poets, by imitation, might achieve the greatness achieved by Homer—and of course by Virgil too. In short, the neoclassicist cared little whether the *Iliad* was an ancient or recent poem, or was an adequate or inadequate expression of the Homeric age. To him the important ques-

tion was whether it, or any other poem, was still a vital experience
to the sensitive reader or whether it was a hollow thing of temporary value at best.

Logically, then, the neoclassicist and the critic who used only a
historical approach would seem to be at opposite poles, the one seeking the unchanging elements of poetry, the other trying to identify
the elements which are constantly changing. In practice the contrast
is not quite so sharp, for the neoclassicist did make historical comments. It must not be thought that a writer like M. Dacier could
do nothing but draw up rules for aspiring poets to use, that he kept
Homer's poems in a kind of vacuum, as it were, never once considering that a man wrote the *Iliad* and that he wrote it in a certain period
of history. For, as the seventeenth century progressed, critics began
to consider, in addition to the rules for the formation of an epic, the
mental qualifications of the poet himself. They spoke of "wit" and
"judgment," defining what they were and indicating their relation
to one another.[1] More than once the question was raised: how did
Homer write so well before the discovery of the rules of art?
He copied nature, came the answer, or, as M. Dacier believed, he
achieved perfection "par la seule force de son génie," or, again, he
possessed remarkable judgment, enabling him to do that which inferior spirits can only accomplish by following the stipulated rules.
While this may seem like rather superficial criticism, it does show
that even among the neoclassicists there was a growing tendency to
remove the work of art from its vacuum. The critic considers the
poem in connection with the poet. A few steps further and the critic
will consider also the environment in which the poet wrote and its
effect upon his work.

Those steps were rarely taken, and then only with the greatest hesi-
tation. The translator of Le Bossu, for example, says that the times
in which Homer lived are so obscure that we can learn next to nothing about him. We only know that he was a wandering bard, "as Poor
as he was Ingenious," who received no greater rewards for his efforts than a few promises which were never kept.[2] M. Dacier, as
staunch a neoclassicist as any, occasionally apologizes for Homer
and Virgil by pointing to the age in which each lived. If Virgil is
more conservative in the use of the marvelous, he says, it is because
"ce qui étoit admirable dans le siecle d'Homere auroit pû être mal
receu dans celuy d'Auguste."[3] Concerning the manners of Homer's

1. An excellent example of this type of criticism may be found in Dryden's preface
to the *Fables*. He considers the "genius" and "judgment" and the "natural inclinations"
of Homer and Virgil. *Essays of John Dryden*, W. P. Ker, ed. (Oxford, 1900), II, 251.
2. *Monsieur Bossu's Treatise of the Epick Poem*, "W.J.," tr. (London, 1695), Preface.
3. André Dacier, *La Poëtique d'Aristotle, traduite en François, avec des remarques*
(Paris, 1692), p. 400. Cf. Bossu, *op. cit.*, p. 139. He says "that which is a Beauty in

heroes, the critics are usually reticent. Rapin is rather indignant because Homer allows Ulysses to be unfaithful to his wife, spending "so long a time in the dalliances of his Prostitute *Calypso*."[4] But a moment later he adds that Homer's weakness must be pardoned, for he "writ in a time when Morality was hardly come to any perfection."[5] Virgil had a great advantage over Homer in this respect: in Homer's "primitive times" there were only such heroes as Hercules and Theseus, reputed for strength rather than virtue, from whom the poet could copy. That their own passions were their worst enemies, and not their opponents on the field of battle, the early poets could not be expected to know.[6]

But a search for remarks of this kind in the works of the seventeenth-century neoclassicists yields little fruit. Once they are found, it is obvious that such passages are isolated from the author's main argument and that a moment later the discussion of rules will be resumed. Nothing approaching real historical perspective is found, therefore, until one turns to the famed Battle of Ancients and Moderns. In the literary part of the quarrel, the Moderns made much of the distinction between the organic and the inorganic. They insisted that the principle of growth and change had always dominated political society and that man had made a gradual but certain progress from a passionate to a rational being. In religion, in ethics, in all things human, this principle had operated, and it must have operated just as surely in literature too. There was no reason to believe that literature had been unique in its development, that it could have suddenly reached maturity while society was still in its infancy. History revealed that men in Homer's time lived in an imperfect, nearly barbaric society: poetry of that time must therefore have been imperfect and nearly barbaric. It was as crude compared to Roman poetry as Roman poetry was crude compared to modern French or English poetry. But the Moderns did not use history alone to prove that poetry had become, with several retrogressions, steadily better. Poetry proved the point too. Close inspection of content—many of these inspections were made—showed that the earlier the poem, the more primitive the actions, manners, and customs described in it.

As long as the Moderns were content to speak broadly of literature in connection with history, the reputation of Homer was not seriously endangered. But during the eighties and nineties he was selected as the target for general attack, as the prime example of the barbaric poet. Virgil, having lived slightly later than Homer, seemed

---

Homer, might have met with sorry Entertainment in the Works of a Poet in the days of Augustus."

4. R. Rapin, *Observations on the Poems of Homer and Virgil*, John Davies, tr. (London, n.d.), p. 55.

5. *Idem*, p. 57.　　　　　　　　6. *Idem*, p. 19.

only slightly more refined. As Perrault says, in comparing the works of the two poets, "Autant que ceux du premier [Homer], quoy qu'admirables en certains endroits, me paroissent pleins de grossiereté, de puerilité, & d'extravagance; autant ceux du dernier me semblent remplis de finesse, de gravité, & de raison: ce qui ne vient que de la différence des temps où ils ont écrit, & de ce que Virgile est plus moderne qu'Homére de huit ou neuf cens ans."[7] Even though he did not believe that any age has a monopoly upon genius, Fontenelle was also obsessed by this idea that civilization and literature had steadily progressed down to modern times. One prefers Virgil to Homer, he says, Horace to Pindar, and the age of Augustus to ancient Greece, because "cet ordre est fort naturel." Time, change, development made anything Greek inferior to anything Roman—at least in the realm of literature.[8]

Slightly more complex are the arguments of John Dennis in "The Advancement and Reformation of Modern Poetry." The early Greeks, he says, imagined every field and grove full of deities of various kinds, all exercising great power over human life. So great was their superstition that they believed one god or another had a hand in almost every event that took place. In this religious environment, so favorable to imaginative poetry, Homer wrote his epic poems.[9] One naturally expects Dennis to maintain that the Greek bard was consequently much superior to all later writers and to anyone who might come hereafter. Instead, he falls in line with the progressivists. While Homer appealed solely to the passions of men,[1] Virgil, in a more advanced age, knew "that the Reason must find its Account in Poetry, as well as the Passions and the Senses."[2] The Æneid proves that he understood this, and is hence a more pleasing poem to us than either the Iliad or the Odyssey. But Dennis was not content in supporting the views of the "rationalists." He also took sides in the quarrel over Christian versus pagan poetry. While Greek superstition may have inspired Homer, the discovery of the true religion and the further

7. Charles Perrault, *Paralelle des anciens et des modernes, en ce qui regarde les arts et les sciences* (Paris, 1693), II, 86–7.

8. "Digression sur les anciens et les modernes," in *Oeuvres de Monsieur de Fontenelle* (Paris, 1752), IV, 185.

9. *The Critical Works of John Dennis*, E. N. Hooker, ed. (Baltimore, 1939), I, 236. Dennis asks, "But since these Visions, and these Apparitions, join'd to their constant Reading the Poets, had such a mighty Influence upon the People, what must they not have had upon their Priests the Poets?"

1. Dennis says Homer "writ to the People of his own Age, in which the Reason of Mankind was satisfy'd at an easier Rate." *Idem*, I, 265.

2. *Ibid*. Dennis explains: "I do not pretend at the same Time, that *Virgil* is capable of giving us a greater Pleasure than *Homer* gave his Contemporaries. As likewise when I affirm, that the Moderns, by joining Poetry with the True Religion, will have the Advantage of the Ancients, I mean only in regard to us."

development of moral principles have given modern poets an advantage which Homer and other ancient poets never had.

Through discussions of this kind, it is easy to see that Homer was being pushed back further and further into the past, that he was being viewed less as a kind of "venerable modern" and more as a poet of a very early age, recording the ideas and manners of that age. Rejecting him as a mine of every branch of knowledge,[3] as a familiar friend and guide, the Moderns suddenly became aware that they did not understand him at all. Because of the immense changes which had come about in the development of society, they felt that they were obliged to exert themselves to arrive at a full comprehension of the Homeric poems. As Le Clerc says, agreeing with the Moderns, "Il faut, pour ainsi dire, transplanter son esprit dans les siecles passez, afin de prendre leur goût & leurs maniéres."[4] Had critics been willing to follow this suggestion without prejudice, there might have been less distaste for Homer. He might have been more widely appreciated than ever. But the Modern of course had little use for anything belonging to the past, and Homer, he said, was obviously a poet of a distant day.

As one might expect, a frequently agitated question at this time was that of the identity of Homer, a question which had descended to the seventeenth century from antiquity. It had received its first important expression in the works of literary critics in Rapin's *Observations*. He had quoted Aelian as saying that Homer had created his epics as a group of individual episodes which were brought to Athens by Lycurgus and molded into complete poems at the order of Pisistratus. Rapin had not believed the story, apparently because he felt that it would deprive Homer of a large share of his glory.[5] In his essay, "Of Poetry" (1690), William Temple speaks of Lycurgus as a great lover of literature, to whom "we are said by some Authors to owe the Collection and Preservation of the loose and scattered Pieces of *Homer* in the Order wherein they have since appeared."[6] It is obvious, from the casual way in which he deals with the matter, that Temple was not in the least alarmed by the reports of these au-

---

3. In his *Paralelle*, ii, 53, Perrault says, "Rien n'est moins vray, qu'Homère ait sçû les Arts." Perrault stated that Homer had erroneously placed the island of Syros in the tropics instead of the Mediterranean; that he further proved his ignorance by having Ulysses' dog recognize his master after twenty years, for the life of a dog is considerably shorter than that. *Idem*, ii, 63 ff.

4. Theodore Parrhase (Jean Le Clerc), *Parrhasiana, ou pensées diverses sur des matiéres de critique, d'histoire, de morale et de politique* (Amsterdam, 1701), i, 7.

5. Rapin, *op. cit.*, p. 114. Rapin adds, "I find in myself a backwardness to assent to this story." *Idem*, p. 115.

6. *Critical Essays of the Seventeenth Century*, J. E. Spingarn, ed. (Oxford, 1909), iii, 107.

thors. That the *Iliad* and *Odyssey* might not have been written by Homer or that there may never have been a Homer did not occur to him any more than it had occurred to Rapin.[7]

But inferences of this nature were subsequently drawn by the zealous Perrault in 1693. He said "qu'il n'y a jamais eu au monde un homme nommé Homére."[8] Instead of one great epic poet, there were dozens of such poets among the ancient Greeks, writing perhaps twenty or thirty short episodes every year, the large majority of which treated the ever-popular subject of the Trojan War.[9] The best of these "petits poëmes" were then joined together and called "rhapsodies," a Greek term, according to Perrault, signifying "un amas de plusieurs chansons cousües ensemble."[1] Supposing this to have been the true origin of the Homeric poems, we can begin to see why so many cities contended for the honor of being Homer's birthplace, each city having, as it were, its own Homer.[2] Logical as this argument may have seemed to him, Perrault realized that he was here expressing heretical opinions. Unwilling to defend his contention, he changed his position and concluded that, if a Homer did exist, "je suis persuadé qu'Homére n'a eu d'autre intention que d'écrire la guerre des Grecs contre les Troyens . . . ; le tout par piéces & par morceaux indépendans les uns des autres."[3]

The language of Homer was another subject for investigation. In his essay, "Of Poetry," Temple speculated whether verse developed prior to prose, concluding that Homer lived several hundred years before Pherecides, the first prose writer.[4] Wotton went a little further. Attributing some of the ancients' success to genius, he says, "yet the Language it self had so great an Influence, that if *Homer* and *Virgil* had been *Polanders* or *High-Dutch*-Men, they would never in all probability have thought it worth their while to attempt the Writing of Heroick Poems."[5] Homer was perhaps the more fortunate of the two. Because the Greek language was so remarkably smooth and expressive, the people were delighted by poetry and paid the highest respect to those who could create it. Rivalry became keen among the bards. Urged on in this manner, it was natural that "here and

---

7. Many authors of the time agreed that Homer was not the first epic poet of Greece. Richard Blackmore, in his preface to *Prince Arthur,* says that Aristotle "tells us of an Epick Poem, intituled, *The Little Ilias,* and another, the *Cyprica." Idem,* III, 241.

8. Perrault, *op. cit.,* II, 23.   9. *Ibid.*

1. *Idem,* II, 24.   2. *Idem,* II, 177.

3. *Idem,* II, 32. Perrault pointed out that D'Aubignac had prepared a book to prove these ideas about the authorship of the Homeric poems. As we shall see, Perrault's position is very similar to that taken by D'Aubignac in his *Conjectures académiques ou dissertation sur l'Iliade,* first published in 1715 but written before Perrault's *Paralelle* appeared.

4. Spingarn, *op. cit.,* III, 86.

5. "Reflections upon Ancient and Modern Learning," in *idem,* III, 210.

there some, one or two at least of a sort, proved excellent."[6] Homer
was one of these few. Another critic, Fontenelle, while condemning
the Greek poet for mingling so many dialects in his epics, says that
in Homer's time it was "une grande merveille qu'un Homme pût assu-
jettir son discours à des mesures, à des sillabes longues & breves, &
faire en même temps quelque chose de raisonnable."[7] It would indeed be surprising if Perrault had nothing to add about Homeric
language. But he had. He objected to the application of certain mean
or coarse phrases to such heroic characters as Hector and Achilles.[8]
This weak criticism stirred up Boileau, who replied with the just observation that "les mots des langues ne répondent pas toujours juste
les uns aux autres."[9] Giving as an example the French word "ane," he
tried to show how favorably its equivalent in Greek was received by
men in Homer's time. The ancient bards cannot be blamed because
a word translated literally into French retains none of its ancient
dignity.[1]

Homeric language, however, caused far less argument than Homeric characters. From the Moderns came the complaint that the
heroes of the *Iliad* were mere barbarians and were clearly not, as
some critics had claimed, perfect examples for all men to follow.
Achilles is too brutal and impetuous, they said; a hero should be a
gentleman, someone to be admired.[2] A few defenders came to
Homer's rescue, arguing that the warriors of Greece and Troy could
hardly be expected to behave like Frenchmen. But no one had so
much to say about Homeric manners or gave them such genuine
historical treatment as St. Evremond in his remarkable essay, "Sur
les poëmes des anciens." Since this work constitutes an important
step in the development of the criticism of Homer and is not merely
another vicious attack upon the "barbarous" past, one is well repaid
in examining it in some detail.

St. Evremond's argument proceeds after this fashion: the early epic
poets are to be greatly admired, deserving to be read with the utmost
care. One must not assume, however, that they should be imitated
or held up as the most perfect writers of all times, for "le changement
de la religion, du gouvernement, des moeurs, des manières"[3] has been

6. *Idem*, III, 206. 7. *Fontenelle, op. cit.*, IV, 193.
8. An example of Perrault's objection: "Agamemnon dit à Ulysse, qu'il fut assommé
comme un boeuf par Egiste; & que ceux qui l'accompagnoient furent tuez comme des
cochons qu'un homme riche fait tuer pour une nopce, ou pour une feste." Perrault,
op. cit., II, 59.
9. *Oeuvres de Boileau*, M. Amar, ed. (Paris, 1811), III, 258.
1. *Idem*, III, 259. Boileau asks, "Prendrons-nous le parti d'accuser Homère et
Virgile, de bassesse, pour n'avoir pas prévu que ces termes, quoique si nobles et si doux
à l'oreille en leur langue, seroient bas et grossiers, étant traduits un jour en françois?"
2. Perrault did not object to Nausicaa's journey to the river on wash-day, but
Achilles' treatment of Agamemnon distressed him. See Perrault, *op. cit.*, II, 34.
3. *Oeuvres mêlées de Saint-Evremond*, Charles Giraud, ed. (Paris, 1865), II, 492.

considerable enough since Homer's time to alter many of our theories of epic poetry. For example, some critics do not think the system of ancient religion essential to early poems, but, if one should remove the deities from the *Iliad*, there would be no *Iliad* any longer.[4] Similarly, the manners of men are very different from what they were in ancient Greece. That Homer may have revealed to his readers some of the unalterable characteristics of human nature is a fact which cannot be controverted. On the other hand, "Homère a plus songé à peindre la nature telle qu'il la voyoit, qu'à faire des héros fort accomplis,"[5] as we might well expect him to do. In that early society he found men governed largely by passion, with no real knowledge of the distinction between good and evil. Is there any reason, then, why he would not give his characters "plus de passions que de vertus?"[6] Is there any reason why Achilles would not have great courage and friendship, and at the same time a "nature incertaine et mal réglée" which manifested itself in barbarous and childish actions?[7]

Turning to the matter of ancient customs, St. Evremond says that, although warriors no longer weary one another by reciting their genealogies before coming to blows, this was the practice in Homer's age: "On discouroit, avant que de se battre, comme on harangue, en Angleterre, avant que de mourir."[8] Nor can we object to the relation of falsehoods in the Homeric poems, for "un mensonge utile, une fausseté heureuse, faisoit l'interêt des imposteurs, et le plaisir des crédules. C'étoit le secret des grands et des sages, pour gouverner les peuples et les simples."[9] At that time men did not seek the truth, or preferred, at least, to have it veiled by allegory. Reality was consequently hidden beneath images and fables by every poet who wished to please.[1] Had St. Evremond gone just a little further at this point, he might have shown how this love for allegory prevailed in more recent times in western Europe. But pointing out the similarities between romance and ancient epic was a task left for Richard Hurd and Clara Reeve a century later.

St. Evremond, then, stands out as an exception—as almost the only critic to use the new approach with anything like impartiality, merely to explain Homeric backgrounds. There are good reasons why he was an exception. It is obvious that many of the Ancients, faithful to Homer, were still placing their faith on the authority of Aristotle and were vigorously defending the poet's greatness with traditional argu-

4. *Idem*, II, 493. He says, "Sans la prière de Thétis à Jupiter, et le songe que Jupiter envoie à Agamemnon, il n'y a point d'ILIADE."

5. *Idem*, II, 496.   6. *Idem*, II, 497.

7. *Ibid*.   8. *Idem*, II, 497–8.

9. *Idem*, II, 500.

1. Blackmore says, in his preface to *Prince Arthur*, "great use was made by Learned and Wise Men of these *feign'd Discourses, Fables*, or *Apologues*, to teach the ruder and more unpolish'd Part of Mankind." Spingarn, *op. cit.*, III, 235.

ments about his permanent values, moral lessons, and the "form" of the *Iliad* and *Odyssey*. They did use history, of course. They used it to explain certain difficult passages in Homer or to substantiate the age-old excuses for the barbarity of his characters. More important, the Ancients—as the term "Ancients" suggests—were intent upon proving that in literature especially, or in certain types of literature, perfection had been attained only in the distant past. They were usually dogmatists, glorifying Greece or Rome or both, the heroic ages, or the epic, at the expense of other countries, ages, or types of literature.

The Moderns were equally dogmatic, equally vigorous in justifying a point of view. While they often insisted that the critical methods and standards applied to Homer could not, for historical reasons, be applied to Tasso or recent poets, they clearly had no intention of setting up relative standards, of finding Homer and Tasso equally good by different sets of criteria. Nor did they wish to support the point of view of the later historical critic that the poems of Homer, Virgil, or Tasso were good only insofar as they "expressed" the ages in which they were written. Relative criticism, of any kind, would make acceptable many poets of many ages, each in his own right, and the Modern, of course, believed only in the Moderns. He therefore used history to demonstrate their greatness. He pointed out that a poem is a basically unique portrayal of a given age, as indeed the historical critic would agree with him, and that criticism should regard in detail the close relation between the age and its poetry. Poetry was visualized as an "expression" of the age. It was this connection between the two, in fact, that seems to have warranted the Modern's belief that society and literature have advanced together and that the best poetry could emerge only from the most advanced age. To many Frenchmen there was little doubt that there was no more civilized country than the France of Louis XIV or that the poetry of all other nations and times was inferior to modern French poetry. French poetry was rational and Christian; Homer's was passionate and pagan.

Obviously there was no historical criticism in this struggle. Only when standards are thoroughly relative can we have historical criticism, only when one has decided that a poem does or does not reflect the main features of the life and thought of an age and one has then estimated the poem's value on the basis of this decision. Nevertheless, the Battle did a great deal toward ending once and for all the belief that literature could be understood adequately without going into historical backgrounds. The struggle as a whole, not merely the literary part of it, made this contribution. It emphasized uniqueness, differences, change, and development, not permanence or universality. "Decorum" and "costume," to which earlier neoclassicists had often paid attention only in passing, became all-important, and Homer and Virgil, however different they may have seemed formerly, now seemed more different than ever. Comparison between them and recent poets appeared almost impossible, for similarities were hard to find. In short, the Battle prepared the way for new developments in criticism. It at least brought about an awareness of a past and present, in literature as in other things, and this awareness was to have far-reaching effects upon eighteenth-century interpretations of Homer and of all poets.

II

Early Eighteenth Century

DURING the first decades of the eighteenth century it became increasingly apparent that a defense of Homer, or of any poet, merely by an application of neoclassical principles, was not likely to receive much sympathy. To try fully to account for this fact would naturally lead one far afield. But a strictly neoclassic type of criticism had never been very popular in England, and in both England and France wider historical perspective and greater interest in the psychology of the poet were at least partly responsible for the growing scarcity of criticism such as that of M. Dacier. To be sure, while Addison tested *Paradise Lost* by neoclassic criteria, his examination was scarcely as rigorous and detailed as the typical formal essay of the preceding century. Milton's sublimity of thought and expression received far more attention than his conformity to the rules. The same kind of treatment was afforded Homer. Accepting the unity of the *Iliad* and *Odyssey*, Addison was mainly concerned with showing how the Greek poet creates sublime ideas and images, how he rises above other poets in his use of the marvellous and in making each of his characters a distinct and interesting personality. Similarly, Pope emphasized Homer's genius for invention rather than his intuitive understanding of the rules of epic poetry. "On whatever side we contemplate *Homer*," he says, "what principally strikes us is his *Invention*."[1] Other writers went a step beyond the moderate neoclassicists and entirely rejected Aristotelian criticism. The beauties of poetry, Welsted declared, "are of too fine and subtle an Essence, to fall under the Discussion of Pedants, Commentators, or trading Criticks": poetry must be felt, not analyzed.[2]

Coincident with the development of new approaches to literature was an increasing enthusiasm for poets and poems more or less scorned by the earlier supporters of Homer. In France La Motte extended the genre of the epic to include *Clovis*, the *Lutrin*, *Pharsale*, and the prose romance—all rather strange company for the *Iliad*. Even Addison was convinced that the rules of Aristotle "cannot be supposed to quadrate exactly with the heroic Poems which have been made since his Time."[3] Hughes's edition of Spenser and especially his

1. *The Iliad of Homer*, Alexander Pope, tr. (London, 1715–20), I, Preface.
2. "A Dissertation Concerning the Perfection of the English Language," in *Critical Essays of the Eighteenth Century*, W. H. Durham, ed. (New Haven, 1915), p. 365.
3. *The Spectator*, G. Gregory Smith, ed. (London, 1907), Vol. II, No. 273, p. 86.

preface to that work (1715), Addison's enthusiasm for Milton and for *Chevy Chase,* the growing interest in Tasso and the poetic parts of the Bible all indicated that the attention of French and English critics was turning away from Homer and Virgil and that these critics were discovering new rivals for the ancient poets.[4]

While this was the new direction in which criticism was moving, the high reputation of Homer substantially remained and Aristotelian criticism of his works continued, in one form or another, during the entire eighteenth century. In fact, in the opening years of that century the Moderns answered those of the Ancients who used neoclassic rules in defending Homer by demonstrating that Homer's works did not have the primary requisite for the epic poem, a carefully contrived design. Hence writers like Terrasson endeavored to prove by "reason" that Homer was inconsistent, that he digressed in one place and repeated himself in another, that the episodical nature of the *Iliad* proved he was only an idle teller of tales. But, whether or not a critic depended primarily on formal criticism, whether he argued for or against Homer, one thing was certain: he could not ignore, as he might have done formerly, the fact that the *Iliad* and *Odyssey* were written in an early period of civilization and bore the marks of that period. So much emphasis had been placed upon the particular rather than the universal elements of Homer's poetry that it was no longer possible to avoid a certain amount of historical interpretation. Particularly against those who drew contrasts between the barbarity of Homeric manners and the refinement of modern manners, the "rules" did not appear appropriate weapons. What was the use of continuing to cite Aristotle, when a man as cold and calculating as Terrasson declared, "I have shew'd in the following Work, that *Homer,* even with respect to his own Age and Time, is highly worthy of Blame, and obnoxious on many Accounts"?[5] Even with respect to his age and time! This was a direct challenge. The moment had arrived for someone to accept that challenge by using the historical approach in Homer's defense.

The Battle of the Ancients and Moderns had subsided into nothing more than desultory sniping when Mme. Dacier published her prose translation of the *Iliad.* Disgusted with the progressivists, tired of

4. Addison found Milton's action greater than Homer's. *Idem,* Vol. II, No. 267, pp. 62–3. He considered some parts of the Old Testament "more elevated and sublime than any in *Homer." Idem,* Vol. 1, No. 160, p. 283.

5. *Critical Dissertations on Homer's Iliad, in a Manner Never Before Attempted, Translated from the French of the Abbé Terrasson* (London, 1745), 1, lxi. Terrasson asks, "Why should he have embraced or adopted popular Errors and Opinions, with all their Absurdities and Impiety? Could he neither rectify nor improve them?" *Idem,* II, 77. Terrasson also objected to Homer because he was not a good teacher of "morality." He preferred *Télémaque* to Homer's works because it showed how a great prince is formed.

hearing how the Greeks *should* have written, this lady came forth as an uncompromising champion of Homer, prepared and eager to defend him from every possible charge. It is doubtful whether the Greek poet has ever had so ardent an admirer. But it was precisely this beatification of Homer, this unwillingness to admit that he had ever sinned,[6] that brought down the indignation of Houdar La Motte upon her head—and consequently opened the second phase of the controversy.

Though Mme. Dacier had the greatest respect for the neoclassical approach and found frequent occasion to use it, she was apparently the first to make a systematic defense of Homer by means of the historical approach. In so doing she blazed a trail upon which Pope and his partners were soon to follow. Why discuss how Homer ought to have written, she argued, when most people do not know how he has written? If times have changed so greatly since the early ages of Greece, why not try to understand how those times affected the *Iliad* instead of expecting the poet to conform to our ideas? "Homere ne pouvoit pas se conformer aux usages des siecles suivants; & c'est aux siecles suivants à remonter aux usages de son siecle."[7] He could only copy nature as he found it at that particular time.[8]

Precisely what Mme. Dacier and her followers thought of the heroic age is often difficult to determine. As far as the customs described by Homer are concerned, everyone applauded them as indicative of the simplicity of life in the early ages of the world. But no one seems to have made an earnest attempt to reconcile, by means of historical study, the ferocious manners of the *Iliad* and the peaceful, domestic ones of the *Odyssey*, or to determine which were representative of Homer's time. So enthusiastic was Mme. Dacier, at least, that she almost overlooked the inhuman behavior of Achilles and Ajax. She emphasizes "la simplicité des moeurs heroiques" and nature "dans sa premiere simplicité"[9] but scarcely says a word about the way in which Hector's body was dragged around the city of Troy. Apparently assuming that a study of customs, not manners, is the best means to arrive at an understanding of early society, she explains in great detail how princes prepared food, how they killed, cleaned,

6. Anne Dacier, *L'Iliade d'Homere, traduite en françois, avec des remarques* (Paris 1711), I, xxiv.
7. *Ibid.*
8. In justifying the use of prose instead of verse in her translation, Mme. Dacier declares that her one aim is to reveal Homer as he really is: "ce n'est pas Homere vivant & animé, je l'avouë, mais c'est Homere." *Idem,* I, xxxvii. When one uses verse, "il faut necessairement qu'il change, qu'il retranche, qu'il adjouste." *Idem,* I, xxxviii.
9. "Homere peint par tout la Nature telle qu'elle estoit dans sa premiere simplicité, & avant que dechuë de sa dignité & de sa noblesse, elle eust cherché à estayer ses ruines sur une pompe vaine, qui n'est jamais la marque d'une veritable & solide grandeur." *Idem,* I, xxiii.

and roasted an animal on spits, and tells her readers that this was the custom "de ces heureux temps où l'on ne connoissoit ni le luxe ni la molesse, & où l'on ne faisoit consister la gloire que dans le travail & dans la vertu."[1] In concluding, she leaves no doubt that she had accepted the challenge of the Moderns and was ready to use the same weapons they were using: "Pour moy, . . . je trouve ces temps anciens d'autant plus beaux, qu'ils ressemblent moins au nostre."[2]

Another writer who took somewhat the same view of the Homeric age was Fénelon. He paid high tribute to the friendship and hospitality of the Greeks. "Rien n'est si aimable que cette vie des premiers hommes."[3] "Cette simplicité de moeurs semble ramener l'âge d'or."[4] As his *Télémaque* bears witness, Fénelon views Greek civilization in the time of Homer as the "youth of mankind," when there was little of the luxury of the modern age. But, unlike Mme. Dacier, Fénelon also finds reason to object to Homeric Greece. He is displeased by its warlike spirit and its savageness, by heroes like Achilles who "ne ressemblent point à d'honnêtes gens."[5] In fact, Virgil or Horace would seem more to Fénelon's taste than Homer.[6]

Addison, in turn, admits that many of Homer's sentiments seem indelicate to modern readers, hastening to add that all "defects" of this kind may be attributed to the age rather than the poet. But, however one may object to the *Iliad* and *Odyssey* on this account, there is nothing more pleasurable than reading works which portray ancient manners and human nature in its primeval simplicity. In turning one's view from the polished, refined characters in modern poems to the heroes of antiquity, "you would think you were reading the History of another Species."[7]

La Motte, Mme. Dacier's opponent, discusses all aspects of the Homeric age. Instead of ignoring anything that seems barbaric and calling attention only to customs and a few more simple, naïve manners, he declares that customs and manners must be distinguished and their relative importance discovered. Agreeing that "l'innocente simplicite des moeurs" in Homer's poems is truly admirable, that nobody can object to seeing kings cook meat and dress themselves without a valet, La Motte says it is scarcely possible to feel sympa-

---

1. *Idem*, I, xxvi–xxvii.   2. *Idem*, I, xxv.
3. *Lettre sur les occupations de l'Academie Française suivie des lettres de Lamotte et de Fénelon sur Homère et sur les anciens*, M. E. Depois, ed. (Paris, n.d.), p. 107.
4. *Idem*, p. 50.   5. *Idem*, p. 103.
6. As with Mme. Dacier, customs are more highly praised than manners. Fénelon calls special attention to "les occupations de Nausicaa," which he contrasts with the customs of the present age. See *idem*, pp. 108–09.
7. Smith, *op. cit.*, Vol. II, No. 209, p. 153. Addison says, "If we look into the Manners of the most remote Ages of the World, we discover Human Nature in her Simplicity; and the more we come downward towards our own Times, may observe her hiding herself in Artifices and Refinements, Polished insensibly out of her Original Plainness."

thetic toward the manners of the Homeric hero. What other term than barbarous can be applied to the behavior of Agamemnon and Achilles, when we observe them constantly wrangling to see who can gain possession of a female slave? But this does not mean that the poet must be condemned. We must differentiate between the author and the age in which he lives, his genius and the materials upon which it works. At a time when "la vengeance & l'orgueil étoient en honneur,"[8] when Greece was little more than a village compared to modern society, it is not strange that the poet should have given his heroes the qualities of fierce and vigorous rustics. Neither Homer nor his audience could imagine heroes of any other type.[9] For that reason, he says, "Le plus grand vice d'Homere . . . est donc d'être né dans un siécle grossier,"[1] and the *Iliad* "me paroît aussi éloigné de la perfection, que l'Auteur étoit propre à l'atteindre, s'il êut été placé dans les bons siécles."[2]

As far as Homeric customs are concerned, Pope was in complete agreement with Mme. Dacier and he paid tribute to her by incorporating a large number of her remarks on that subject in the "Observations" which follow each book of his translation. Anyone who reads Homer should realize that he is becoming acquainted with "the most ancient Author in the Heathen World," says Pope; he should realize that he is "stepping almost three thousand Years backward into the remotest Antiquity."[3] Unless he looks upon the customs of the *Iliad* from a historical point of view and studies the meaning of them closely, "no Man can tolerably understand this Author."[4] Pope considered it unreasonable to take the attitude of some modern critics: to scoff when Homer represents princes tending their flocks and supervising their harvests, when he describes princesses drawing water for the royal household and kings dining in the open about a campfire.[5] "There is a Pleasure in taking a view of that Simplicity in Opposition to the Luxury of succeeding Ages."[6] But, much as he

8. "Discours sur Homère," in *Oeuvres de Monsieur Houdar de La Motte* (Paris, 1754), II, 94.
9. La Motte says, "Je répons qu'Homere a suivi les idées de son tems, & qu'il portoit des choses les mêmes jugemens que ses auditeurs. Il n'avoit peut-être pas la force de s'élever à des idées plus justes; mais aussi n'étoit-il pas nécessaire pour son dessein. La vengeance & l'orgueil étoient en honneur; il les y a laissées; & son siécle n'étoit point choqué de les voir représenter sous des traits qui confirmoient son jugement." *Ibid.*
1. "Reflexions sur la Critique," in *Oeuvres de Monsieur Houdar de La Motte*, III, 187.
2. "Discours sur Homère," in *Oeuvres de Monsieur Houdar de La Motte*, II, 97.
3. Pope, *op. cit.*, I, Preface.   4. *Idem*, II, 92.
5. Pope says, "It should methinks be a Pleasure to a modern Reader to see how such mighty Men, whose Actions have surviv'd their Persons three thousand Years, liv'd in the earliest Ages of the World." *Idem*, III, 59–60. He also remarks, "The Objections some have made that *Homer's* Gods and Heroes do every thing for themselves, as if several of those Offices were unworthy of them, proceeds from the corrupt Idea of modern Luxury and Grandeur." *Idem*, III, 60.
6. *Idem*, I, Preface.

admired the customs of ancient domestic life, he agreed with La Motte that the manners of the *Iliad* were too barbarous, too indecent to win the sympathy of modern readers. Only a prejudiced person could idealize those times "when a Spirit of Revenge and Cruelty reign'd thro' the World, when no Mercy was shown but for the sake of Lucre."[7] So firmly did Pope and his aides maintain this opinion that we find them explaining all kinds of ancient customs in their notes and defending Homer from charges of barbarism, but not once do they pretend that the heroic ages were civilized to any considerable degree.

In these various discussions two things are evident. In the first place, idealists like Mme. Dacier always emphasized early customs and the manners of men at peace, while those who characterized Homer's time as rude spoke of the manners of men at war. A complete picture of the period was lacking. Secondly, the early eighteenth-century critic rarely made a sharp distinction between the age of heroes and the age of Homer. Though they did not think that Homer and Ulysses were contemporaries, they assumed, no doubt, that the passage of two or three hundred years would not be enough to alter perceptibly the customs and manners of men.[8] Instead of attributing the brutality of Achilles to Homer himself or to the condition of society at the time of the Trojan War, most writers blamed the period when the two epics were written. Both Homer and his poems were therefore considered representative of a time either of rudeness or of happy simplicity, according to the interpretation of the individual critic. If, judging by the manners, the age was considered barbarous, so were the poet and his epics; if, judging by the customs, it was considered simple and naïve, so were they.

Again and again, in the first years of the century, arose the problem of Homer's identity and, consequently, of the origin of the *Iliad* and *Odyssey*. Though it never became a focal point in the controversy of Ancients and Moderns, the question worried critics on both sides, particularly those who were unwilling to ascribe repetitions, digressions, and inconsistencies to the poet's lack of genius. Mme. Dacier did not once doubt that Homer was the author of the poems attributed to him but she raised one or two interesting points about the manner in which the *Iliad* and *Odyssey* have come down to modern times. According to the argument of her preface, the epics were both "continus, & nullement divisez par livres" when they were first

7. In one of his notes Pope says, "I think indeed the thing by far the most shocking in this Author, is that Spirit of Cruelty which appears too manifestly in the Iliad." *Idem*, IV, 75.

8. Mme. Dacier says that Homer wrote his poems 250 or 260 years after the Trojan War, and that this was sufficient time to permit a "changement sensible" in the manners of men. Anne Dacier, *op. cit.*, II, 540. But neither she nor any other critic presses the point.

composed.[9] The rhapsodists, however, broke each up into separate episodes, and in this condition they were circulated in Ionia and later throughout Greece. Even after Pisistratus collected the various parts and restored them to their original order in the poems, the rhapsodists continued to sing the tale of the Trojan War by episodes, not infrequently allowing errors to creep in and making interpolations of their own. So much did they and a careless group of copyists depart from the text of Homer that it was again necessary in Alexander's time to revise the two poems.[1]

Thomas Parnell, in his "Essay on Homer," says that "the Works of *Homer* ran the danger of being utterly defac'd" by the insertion of additional passages and by the mistakes made in transcribing the text.[2] But neither for him nor for Mme. Dacier did these facts have any implications. They did not realize, as critics were to realize a hundred years later, that such information could be utilized toward proving the diversity of authorship of the Homeric poems, that the rhapsodists might be directly concerned with the composition of the epics, and that the interpolations, although supposedly removed, might still appear in certain portions of the text. The repeated assurances of all neoclassicists that the *Iliad* and *Odyssey* preserved a remarkable unity of design prevented the important critics of the time from questioning the authorship and the condition of these poems. Hence La Motte confidently answers Perrault and any others who do not believe Homer ever existed: "Je remarque partout dans L'Iliade, les mêmes vûës & la même maniere de penser. . . . L'Iliade est d'un seul Auteur."[3] And Gildon, after summing up the Pisistratus case, says that because of the "Completeness of the Poem," it is obvious "that a certain Rule was propos'd by the *Composer* to himself."[4] No one but Homer could have created so unified a work.

Of all the books treating this subject, D'Aubignac's *Conjectures académiques*[5] is the most important. Written about the middle of the seventeenth century, it was first published in 1715. Many attempts have been made to prove that F. A. Wolf depended upon D'Aubignac for certain arguments in support of his Homeric theory. Whether he did or not, the *Conjectures* anticipates by a hundred years the criticism of Wolf's time. One might safely say that the atti-

---

9. *Idem*, I, lv–lvi.   1. *Idem*, I, lv–lix.
2. "An Essay on the Life, Writings and Learning of Homer," in Pope, *op. cit.*, I, 34.
3. "Discours sur Homère," in *Oeuvres de Monsieur Houdar de La Motte*, II, 2.
4. Charles Gildon, *The Complete Art of Poetry* (London, 1718), I, 97. In this passage Gildon says he does not know "whether the Order and Conduct were the Business of *Lycurgus*, or *Pisistratus*, or any other who collected the scattered Books of that *Poet*, corrected, and first made an Edition of them entire; yet, from the Completeness of the Poem, as together, it is evident, that a certain Rule was propos'd by the *Composer* to himself."
5. François Hédelin, Abbé d'Aubignac, *Conjectures académiques ou dissertation sur l'Iliade*, Victor Magnien, ed. (Paris, 1925). D'Aubignac died about 1676.

tude of the eighteenth century toward Homer would have been altogether different had it not been for one thing: the book was virtually
if not entirely unknown.[6]

Since English critics were in no way influenced by D'Aubignac,
we need only summarize his main argument. Absolutely nothing is
known about Homer, the author says, neither when he was born nor
where, neither what he did nor how he died. Because no historian
until relatively modern times has spoken of him as an individual,
there is every reason to believe the name "Homer" was applied to
any wandering singer. D'Aubignac contends that "rhapsodists" composed songs about the siege of Troy and that various episodes of the
story sung by them were eventually collected and joined together
into a narrative. In order to achieve something like a unity of the
whole, the compiler was obliged to omit certain parts and to add
others of his own invention. But it is still possible to tell where many
of the original episodes began and ended.[7] The French critic then
points out that the repetitions and inconsistencies and the mixture
of the different Greek dialects may be attributed to the diversity of
authorship. Similarly, it is only natural that we should find the rudi-
ments of every art and science in the *Iliad* and *Odyssey*. If many
rhapsodists composed these poems, each included some facts about
his own particular skill or proficiency.[8]

More important to us are the works of several English critics of
the time. In 1713 Henry Felton published his *Dissertation on Reading
the Classics,* a book popular enough to reach a fifth edition by 1753.
Considering the authorship of the Homeric poems he says, "I have
argued hitherto, my Lord, for *Virgil,* and it will be no Wonder, that
his Poem should be more correct in the Rules of Writing, if that
strange Opinion prevaileth, that *Homer* writ without any View or
Design at all, that his Poems are loose, independent Pieces tacked
together, and were originally only so many *Songs* or *Ballads* upon
the *Gods* and *Heroes,* and the *Siege of Troy.*"[9] Like Mme. Dacier and
La Motte, Felton believes the *Iliad* and *Odyssey* are much too well
organized to be compilations of the songs of a mere rhapsodist: "they
are the completest String of Ballads I ever met with."[1] But, if it is

6. Neither Blackwell nor Wood, the two great English Homeric critics of the century,
nor, so far as I know, any of the primitivists ever speaks of the *Conjectures académiques.*

7. Examples of these episodes are: "*Le combat aux Vaisseaux, La valeur d'Agamemnon, La Patroclie, ou L'aventure de Patrocle, Le catalogue des Armées, La rançon
d'Hector . . . ou bien L'antre de Calypso, Les Cyclopes, Les entretiens d'Alcinous.*"
D'Aubignac, *op. cit.,* p. 46.

8. He says, "*Chacun d'eux n'a pas manqué de l'enrichir des choses dont il avait une
parfaite intelligence, soit dans les sciences, soit dans les arts.*" *Idem,* p. 122.

9. Henry Felton, *A Dissertation on Reading the Classics, and Forming a Just Style*
(London, 1753), p. 19.

1. *Ibid.*

true, as many writers claim, that someone in Pisistratus' day assembled the poems of Homer, "let them at least allow us one Poetical Supposition on our side, That *Homer's* Harp was as powerful to command his scattered incoherent Pieces into the beautiful Structure of a Poem, as *Amphion's* was to summon the Stones into a Wall."[2]

Addison would no doubt have agreed with Felton that Homer's poems do not constitute an aggregation of ballads. In discussing the *Iliad* and *Chevy Chase,* he merely points out that both poems grew out of the historical circumstances of the ages in which they were composed.[3] Finding the Greek states threatened by the Persians, Homer sought to conclude the strife among the rulers of those states, to bring about a common front by showing "the several Advantages which the Enemy gained by such their Discords."[4] In the same way the author of *Chevy Chase,* to end the quarrelling of barons with one another and with their neighbors, described a bloody battle "occasioned by the mutual Feuds which reigned in the Families of an *English* and *Scotch* Nobleman."[5]

Such a comparison of the ballad and the epic would be of minor importance to us if critics had not begun to question the accepted ideas about the composition of the *Iliad* and *Odyssey* and therefore to call Homer a rhapsodist or balladist. The remarks of Richard Bentley show to what that comparison might lead. Speaking of Homer, he says, "He wrote a sequel of Songs and Rhapsodies, to be sung by himself for small earnings and good cheer, at Festivals and other days of Merriment."[6] The *Iliad* was composed for men, and the *Odyssey* for women. But neither was "collected together in the form of an Epic poem" until the age of Pisistratus. This explains for Bentley why there is not "one word in *Homer,* that presages or promises Immortality to his work; as we find there is in the later Poets, *Virgil, Horace, Ovid, Lucan,* and *Statius.*"[7]

Equally damaging to the reputation of Homer as a conscious artist is the criticism sometimes wrongly attributed to Ambrose Phillips. *"The very Prince of Poets, old Homer, if we may trust ancient Records, was nothing more than a blind Ballad-singer, who writ Songs of the Siege of Troy, and the Adventures of Ulysses; and playing the Tunes upon his Harp, sung from Door to Door."*[8] Someone

2. *Idem,* p. 23.

3. With the exception of D'Aubignac, who speaks of "cette prétendue guerre de Troie" (D'Aubignac, *op. cit.,* p. 54), every critic agreed that the *Iliad* was based upon historical facts. Speaking of Achilles and Odysseus, Addison says that Homer "has wrought into his two Poems such of their remarkable Adventures as were still talked of among his Contemporaries." Smith, *op. cit.,* Vol. III, No. 351, p. 117.

4. *Idem,* Vol. I, No. 70, p. 265.   5. *Ibid.*

6. Richard Bentley, *Remarks upon a Late Discourse of Free-Thinking: in a Letter to F. H., D.D.* (London, 1716), p. 18.

7. *Ibid.*   8. *A Collection of Old Ballads* (London, 1723), I, iii.

later collected his ballads and "by a little connecting 'em" produced the poems that have come down to us.[9] But this is not all. A few pages later Homer is associated with the balladists of England. It was the custom in ancient Greece for "these Song Enditers" to transmit to posterity the stories of great events which had happened in their own days. "*And I believe it never was used more than amongst the* English *in Times of old.*"[1] Fortunately for Homer, the eighteenth century was not greatly impressed with the comparison.

Much more important were the comparisons between Homer and the Bible. Though often carried too far, they were in part responsible for the development of a historical interpretation of the *Iliad* and *Odyssey*. The Scriptures and the Greek epics, it was realized, were both produced in a very early period and in the same part of the world. Since one finds remarkable similarities of language, manners, and customs, is he not obliged to attribute them to the age, to the climate, or to the intercourse between Hebrews and Greeks rather than to the particular genius of each writer?[2]

The study of these parallels had not been uncommon in the seventeenth century. Mme. Dacier was, however, the first participant in the controversy of Ancients and Moderns to discover how valuable they were in defending Homer. Since we find the same customs described by the Greek poet and by the writers of the Old Testament, she argued, it would be unreasonable to condemn them as barbarous in the one case and give them the highest praise in the other. "Homere parle souvent de chaudrons, de marmites, de sang, de graisse, d'intestins. . . . Les gens du monde trouvent cela choquant; mais on fait voir que tout cela est entierement conforme à ce que l'on voit dans l'Escriture sainte."[3] Why should we think that Nausicaa was abandoning her royal dignity by washing clothes in a river, when the Bible tells us that "les filles les plus considerables," such as Rachel and Rebecca, attended to all sorts of household tasks? Again and again Mme. Dacier concludes her observations on the customs mentioned in the *Iliad* (and *Odyssey*) with the brief statement, "Ce sont ces mesmes moeurs qu'on voit dans l'Escriture sainte."[4]

Even more striking were the similarities in language, in the manner of expression. Speaking of Homer, Mme. Dacier says that "son style est le mesme que celuy qui regne dans les livres des anciens Hebreux."[5]

9. *Idem,* I, iii–iv.   1. *Idem,* I, vii.

2. Since no one would attack the customs or manners described in the Bible, it was of course to the advantage of Homer's defenders to find these similarities.

3. Anne Dacier, *op. cit.,* I, xxvi. Terrasson's reply to Mme. Dacier was that "the Example of the Holy Scriptures don't authorize any Thing, which Reason and the true Rules of Eloquence and Poetry shew to be Faults in *Homer.*" Terrasson, *op. cit.,* II, 226.

4. Anne Dacier, *loc. cit.*

5. *Idem,* I, 431. "Homere donne de l'ame & du mouvement aux choses les plus inanimées; & c'est ce qui donne à ses vers une vie. . . . Tout est animé de mesme dans les livres du vieux Testament. *Idem,* I, 413.

There is a sublimity in both, unequalled by any later writings; and both are inclined to be concise at the same time that they are repetitious. The same figures are used: for example, the comparison of a young warrior to the olive tree. Never quite certain how to account for the many parallels she found, Mme. Dacier sometimes attributes them to the age, at other times to the fact that Homer may have been acquainted with parts of the Old Testament.

Addison thought that a combination of climate and social conditions was responsible for these similarities. In one essay he says that many of "these great natural Genius's, that were never disciplined and broken by Rules of Art," are to be found among the ancients, particularly in "the more Eastern Parts of the World."[6] Living in a time which was unconcerned about "Nicety and Correctness" in poetry, they only tried to achieve a generous likeness in their similes; the "Decency" of the comparison did not trouble them.[7] Hence Solomon finds a resemblance between the nose of his beloved and "the Tower of *Libanon* which looketh toward *Damascus*." Hence, too, Homer compares the angry Achilles to "a Piece of Flesh broiled on the Coals."[8] In a later paper Addison speaks of the "noble spirit of Eastern poetry" in the book of Canticles, "very often not unlike what we meet with in *Homer*, who is generally placed near the Age of *Solomon*."[9] Ezekiel also resembles Homer "in the Poetical Parts of his Prophecy."[1]

Pope, in turn, says "the *Divine Spirit*" used only such words and ideas as were commonly understood by men at the time in which the Scriptures were written. "As *Homer* is the Author nearest to those, his Style must of course bear a greater Resemblance to the sacred Books than that of any other Writer."[2] Sometimes Pope speaks of the *Iliad* in a rather general way, as "very much in the Language of Scripture, and in the Spirit of the Orientals."[3] On other occasions he is more specific: Homer is not only the "oldest Writer in the World except *Moses*" but often expresses himself in the same manner as he.[4] As the locusts in *Exodus* are driven into the sea, so in the *Iliad* are they driven into a river.[5] Digressions, circumlocutions, and dialogue are to be found in both because this was the customary way of writing

6. Smith, *op. cit.*, Vol. II, No. 160, p. 283.   7. *Idem*, Vol. II, No. 160, pp. 283–4.
8. *Idem*, Vol. I, No. 160, p. 284. In another essay Addison points out how Milton imitates the ancients in giving Michael "an Allegorical Weapon" to employ against Satan. "Not only *Homer* has made use of it, but we find the *Jewish* Hero in the Book of *Maccabees*, who had fought the Battels of the chosen People with so much Glory and Success, receiving in his Dream a Sword from the Hand of the Prophet *Jeremiah*." *Idem*, Vol. III, No. 333, p. 48.
9. *Idem*, Vol. III, No. 327, p. 21.   1. *Idem*, Vol. III, No. 333, p. 49.
2. Pope, *op. cit.*, I, Preface. In the same passage Pope says, "This pure and noble Simplicity is no where in such Perfection as in the *Scripture* and our Author."
3. *Idem*, VI, 132.   4. *Idem*, V, 282.
5. *Idem*, V, 283.

among the Greeks and Hebrews of antiquity; and Moses, Homer, and the early writers all used repetitions[6] because they realized that reiterating an idea impressed it more clearly on the minds of their readers.[7]

Mme. Dacier even discovered similarities between Homer's theology and the Hebrew religion and concluded that either Homer came in contact with Jewish doctrines in Egypt or those doctrines had spread to Greece by the time he wrote his poems. Homer believed in immortality, she says, in the existence of "un premier Estre," in a system of rewards and punishments, and in a great many other religious truths recognized by the Hebrews.[8] Once the critics had begun to search for parallels of this kind, they of course found them everywhere. Blackwall asserted that Homer's device of having gods descend to earth to converse with mortals "is copy'd from *God* walking in *Paradise*, and discoursing with our *First Parents*";[9] and Richard Blackmore thought that the heathen writers derived their use of machinery from the book of Job, in which God and "the chief Apostate Angel" are represented as characters opposing one another.[1]

But few critics of importance deigned—or, perhaps, dared—to compare the religious convictions of the Hebrews and of Homer. Writing about the theology of the *Iliad*, some attacked it because it was inferior to Christianity and others defended it by devising elaborate systems of allegory.[2] There was, however, one thing about which everyone agreed: that Homer, in his use of gods and goddesses, did not deviate from the accepted opinions and superstitions of his time. Even Terrasson concedes that "the Ignorance of the Age in

6. Speaking of Homer's repetitions, Pope says: "Far from condemning their frequent Use in the most ancient of all the Poets, we should look upon them as the certain Character of the Age in which he liv'd: They spoke so in his Time, and to have spoken otherwise had been a Fault." *Idem*, v, 183.

7. *Idem*, v, 184.

8. Anne Dacier, *op. cit.*, I, xlviii. Many of the Moderns had raised objections because Homer represented Jove as a deceiver. In defense of the poet, Mme. Dacier says, "L'Escriture sainte nous fournit un exemple tout pareil dans l'histoire d'Achab, Roy d'Israël, quand Dieu voulut le faire perir, car Dieu envoye à ce Roy l'esprit de mensonge pour le séduire. . . . Cet exemple est d'autant plus remarquable, qu'il est du temps mesme d'Homere, car ce poëte vivoit dans le temps qu'Achab estoit Roy d'Israël." *Idem*, I, xxii.

9. Anthony Blackwall, *An Introduction to the Classics* (London, 1737), p. 82.

1. Richard Blackmore, "An Essay on the Nature and Constitution of Epick Poetry," in *Essays upon Several Subjects* (London, 1716), I, 64.

2. Hence Hardouin sought to prove that the divinities of the *Iliad* were either men of different ranks and professions (Vulcan representing the Greek armorers, and Thetis and the sea-deities representing officers of the ships) or that they were human qualities, such as beauty, strength, greatness of soul, etc. Sometimes the divinities represented the various arts, music, navigation, etc. Hardouin devoted an entire book to this subject. See his *Apologie d'Homere, où l'on explique le veritable dessein de son Iliade, & sa theomythologie* (Paris, 1716).

which *Homer* liv'd, and the Darkness of Paganism, with which he was surrounded, render him, in some Measure excusable."[3] La Motte says that, because Homer lived "dans les tems de ténebres," it was impossible for him to avoid "la contagion des erreurs & de l'absurdité du Paganisme."[4] Instead of blaming the poet, as Terrasson does, he makes the people themselves responsible for the extravagance of Homer's theology. To have believed in it, to have accepted it so willingly, they must have been "dans l'imbécillité de l'enfance."[5] Fénelon, pointing out that Homer found a ready-made system of divinities in the theology of his day, says that the poet ornamented but did not alter this system. He described it "avec naïveté, grâce, force, majesté, passion: que veut-on de plus?"[6] In fact, the more monstrous and ridiculous the pagan religion appears to us, the more we ought to admire the way in which Homer has treated it.[7]

It is apparent that the historical approach was not suddenly accepted as the only approach, that other interpretations of literature were equally, if not more, popular in the early years of the eighteenth century. One is not to expect, therefore, a meteoric development of the historical point of view or any appreciable move in the direction of genuine historical criticism. He is not to assume the critics were less dogmatic than before or less violently opposed in their historical interpretations. The Ancients still held to their opinion that literature, perhaps society too, had reached its perfection in the classical world, while the Moderns went on proving that the *Iliad* represented only the rude beginnings of literature. Even in the Moderns' view that Homer and his characters were barbarians, there was little that one could really call original, that had not at least been suggested by earlier critics like Perrault and sometimes by neoclassicists like Scaliger. More specifically, it appears that Bayle's *Dictionaire* was the source for many of the eighteenth-century opinions that Homer's heroes, almost without exception, were shockingly immoral and ill-behaved.[8] Critics in France, England, and Germany repeated over and over again what they had read in Bayle.

3. Terrasson, *op. cit.*, II, 2.
4. "Discours sur Homère," in *Oeuvres de Monsieur Houdar de La Motte*, II, 29.
5. *Idem*, II, 22.
6. Fénelon explains that "Homère a dû, sans doute, peindre ses dieux comme la religion les enseignoit au monde idolâtre en son temps." Depois, *op. cit.*, p. 106.
7. In the same passage, Fénelon says, "Plus la religion étoit monstrueuse et ridicule, plus il faut l'admirer de l'avoir relevée par tant de magnifiques images." *Ibid.*
8. For example, Bayle says of Achilles: "Au reste, le trainement de ce cadavre [Hector], les discours qu'Achille tint à Hector prêt à expirer, la liberté qu'il accorda à qui voulut d'insulter & de fraper ce corps mort, cette ame vénale, qui se laissa enfin persuader, à force de riches présens, de rendre à Priam le corps de son fils, sont des choses si éloignées, je ne dirai pas de la vertu héroïque, mais de la générosité la plus commune, qu'il faut nécessairement juger, ou qu'Homere n'avait aucune idée de l'Héroïsme, ou qu'il n'a eu dessein que de peindre le caractere d'un brutal." Pierre Bayle, *Dictionaire historique et critique* (Amsterdam, 1730), I, 58, n.

At the same time, the second phase of the Battle concerned Homer more directly than did the first one. Views about him were more definitely stated and within limits were more varied than before. To summarize a few of these views, it is certainly doubtful whether anyone had ever gone quite so far as Terrasson when he attempted to show that Homer "even with respect to his own Age and Time, is highly worthy of Blame." Homer was called a barbarian not only because he had lived in a barbarous period but also because, as a poet, he made no effort to rectify the errors and superstitions of his contemporaries. Both Homer and the Homeric age are responsible for the inferiority of the *Iliad*. Mme. Dacier, of course, went to another extreme. She rhapsodized about Homeric society, glorifying its virtues and domestic customs and completely ignoring the fact that the Greeks, as described by Homer, fought bloody wars and treated their enemies with unbelievable cruelty. If Terrasson found nothing good in Homer, Mme. Dacier found nothing bad.

None of the other critics seem to have had such strong feelings toward Homer. La Motte, severe as he may have been, expressed the standard view of the Moderns when he approved of the simple life and picturesque customs of the Greeks but deplored their barbarous qualities. To him Homer was free of blame, a great genius who was unfortunate in having been born in such evil times. Even Fénelon, on the other side of the quarrel, was not so ardent an admirer of Homer or of Homeric generosity and hospitality that he lost sight of certain indications of barbarity among the Greeks. In fact, his tendency to be inconsistent in criticizing Homer is largely owing, I think, to an inability to reconcile the pictures of the Greeks at war with those of the Greeks at peace. Pope, of course, did not try to estimate the Homeric age as thoroughly as any of the four other critics mentioned. But, while he spoke highly of the simplicity of early Greek life (as did Addison), he recognized and disapproved of the warlike spirit and cruelty of Homer's heroes.

Comparisons of Homer and the Bible, Homer and the ballad, discussions of early languages, of the effect of climate upon literary works, and of the origin of Homer's poems—these are all indicative of the development of the historical approach. However, nothing better illustrates this development or more clearly reveals the critic's fundamental attitude toward Homer and his poetry than the way in which estimates of Homeric life are used. On the one hand are writers like Pope who could condemn barbaric heroes while praising Homer. They could do so only because they did not use the historical approach alone, because their evaluations of Homer were not entirely based on content. On the other hand are the critics who viewed literature largely or entirely in terms of historical backgrounds. In most cases this group had already decided whether or not to praise Homer. It was a simple matter then to select certain groups of actions or ideas in the *Iliad* and *Odyssey,* to show that these were or were not barbaric and that therefore Homer was or was not a barbarian. Examination of content alone became the means of justifying, rarely arriving at, an opinion of Homer and his poetry, an opinion which was, in turn, determined by one's attitude toward all early literature. It was not often that a critic accepted Pindar and rejected Homer. If one used history to establish the greatness of Pindar, he usually used it to support Homer and every other ancient poet as well.

While the historical approach was thus employed by each side in the Battle for very different reasons, all the critics of the time had one thing in common. It is interesting to note that no one applauds the primitive aspects of Greek life. The Moderns certainly did not, and the Ancients, even the most fanatic of them, either ignored those aspects or spoke of them with considerable discomfort. The Moderns were thoroughly satisfied with present-day French civilization. The Ancients apparently approved of early man only in his more humane moments when he had no occasion to give free rein to his emotions. They lost interest in him each time that he forsook his simple, quiet occupations for the field of battle. Apparently they yearned for a society that never existed or which at best was realized only in part by the early Greeks. In fact, one suspects that the Ancients were not so dissatisfied with their own age as they often pretended, for a reading of a work like *Télémaque* gives one the impression that they were quite willing to combine many qualities of modern society with a few selected qualities of Homeric society.

III

Thomas Blackwell

BECAUSE he was more interested in the *Iliad* and *Odyssey* as works of art than in Homer the man, the critic in the years before the Battle rarely attempted to disentangle the mass of myths and traditions about Homer which had come down from ancient times. He either apathetically accepted what appeared to him the least inaccurate account or he left all considerations of the poet's biography to the pedant and antiquarian. Ogilby, for instance, printed a summary of Herodotus' life of Homer at the beginning of his translation of the *Iliad* (1669), apparently with the intention of satisfying the curiosity of his readers rather than of giving them a fuller understanding of the poem.

But, with the development of the historical approach at the end of the century, there arose a new interest in biography. Along with general social and cultural backgrounds, it now seemed necessary to study the personal experiences of the poet and to determine how they had affected his works. In the case of Homer it was almost impossible to do this. The only biographical records in existence were those handed down by the ancients, and one had no way of judging their reliability. He was faced with the task of trying to reconcile conflicting accounts or of choosing those which seemed likely and rejecting those which were obviously fictitious.

Nevertheless, three well-known critics of the time—Mme. Dacier, Parnell, and Blackwell—had something new to say about the life of Homer. Mme. Dacier, the first of them in order of time, found that Homer's travels were to a certain extent responsible for his exact descriptions of countries and cities in Asia Minor and Africa, that his visit to Egypt enabled him to learn many things from the priests about the genealogy and occupations of the gods. She was also one of the first critics to revolt against the authority of antiquity, to question parts of the often-quoted biography written by Herodotus. "J'ay naturellement de l'aversion pour tous ces ouvrages où le mensonge a pris la place de la verité."[1] Trying to separate fact from fiction, she wished to give her readers only what appeared "le moins éloigné de la vraysemblance."[2] It seemed to her that an indiscriminate

1. Anne Dacier, "La Vie d'Homere," in *L'Iliade d'Homere, traduite en françois, avec des remarques,* I, 2–3.
2. *Idem,* I, 3.

repetition of dozens of fables concerning Homer was as useless as it was confusing. But, in rejecting some portions of the testimony of the ancients and in accepting others, she seems to have had no particular criterion by which to distinguish the true from the false. She deserves credit, therefore, only because she was so well aware of the possible connections between biography and criticism.

The French "life" was published before the quarrel had entered its important second phase. Parnell's appeared in 1715, at the height of the battle over Homer and after the historical approach had developed to a more advanced stage. One need not be surprised, therefore, that Parnell's version should differ from Mme. Dacier's. Because antiquity has given us so many contradictory stories about Homer, Parnell says, there can be no authoritative biography of the poet.[3] All these accounts—a number are summarized—arise from an "extravagant Indulgence of Fancy." "It looks as if Men imagin'd the Lives of Poets should be Poetically written; that to speak plainly of them, were to speak contemptibly."[4] Showing little mercy for any ancient critic, he is even more willing than Mme. Dacier to discard the information offered by such supposedly reputable authors as Herodotus and Plutarch. The former, he says, writes with "the Spirit of a *Grammarian*," delving into all kinds of particulars of minor importance.[5]

In taking this attitude, Parnell realizes that any discussion of Homer's birth, parentage, and worldly experiences will remain largely speculative: the "Fictions of Poetry" have too often been "converted into real Facts."[6] But the use of internal evidence offers some hope. In turning directly to the *Iliad* and *Odyssey*, Parnell points out that Homer lived long after the siege of Troy because he speaks of the catalogue of ships as something he had heard about through "rumor." Homer's descriptive powers prove that he had not always been blind, as many historians had insisted, and his knowledge of geography and the use of several dialects indicate that he had travelled widely. Internal evidence is again utilized when Parnell attempts to sketch the character of Homer.

In the final section of his "Essay," Parnell goes on to describe the state of society in Homeric times, under such headings as "poetry," "theology," "politics," "morality," and "history." When the poet came into the world, Greece was a "disunited Country" of small states, all of which were constantly at odds; but "whatever was manag'd in War amounted to no more than intestine Skirmishes or Pyracies abroad."[7] Since one was so often obliged to defend himself, strength of body

3. Homer's life, he says, must be "rather spoken of than discover'd." "An Essay on the Life, Writings and Learnings of Homer," in Pope, ed., *The Iliad of Homer*, I, 3.
4. *Idem*, I, 5–6.   5. *Idem*, I, 12.
6. *Idem*, I, 16.   7. *Idem*, I, 46.

was greatly emphasized. "Homer writ for Men," Parnell says, "and therefore he writ of them; . . . we see his People with the turn of his Age, insatiably thirsting after Glory and Plunder."[8] Barbaric in its manners, the time was not much more advanced in its learning. Men were "extreamly ignorant in the Nature of Poetry," the art being confined to "the *Extempore*-Singers of Stories at Banquets."[9] Superstitious in matters of religion, crude in its sentiments, particularly fond of the fabulous, the age obliged Homer to abide by its ideas and to write the kind of poem which would be appreciated by his countrymen.

But Parnell does deserve praise as a Homeric critic. Significant is his conviction that biography must be based solely on fact, not on a mixture of fact and fiction. Nor should his trust in internal evidence be overlooked, a trust which, in the absence of authentic records, most later Homeric critics and scholars were to share with him. Perhaps the most interesting part of his "Essay" is the final section. In discussing the main features of Homer's age—his country and compatriots and the state of society and culture in that time—Parnell becomes one of the first to suggest that a complete picture of historical backgrounds, not a picture based on selected facts, is of considerable value to the reader and student of Homer. In fact, forty or fifty years later the various topics outlined in the "Essay" were to be more and more widely discussed and were to occupy the attention of every critic who used the historical approach.

By far the most important study belonging to the early eighteenth century was Thomas Blackwell's *Enquiry into the Life and Writings of Homer* (1735), parts of which seem to be an elaboration of Parnell's "Essay." To be sure, Blackwell was much less of a skeptic than Parnell, accepting and developing many of the traditions about Homer that had come down from antiquity. But he alone fully realized and proved that the personal experiences of a poet may be responsible for many of the individualities of his poems and that biography should therefore be of the highest importance to critics and scholars. Also to Blackwell's credit is his analysis of Homer's environment, far more searching than Parnell's and one which attracted a great deal of attention later on.

According to the author, the purpose of the *Enquiry* is to discover why, after three thousand years, no one has ever equalled Homer as a composer of epics.[1] He could not believe that the superiority of the Greek poet was owing to a conjunction of the stars or to a divine birth

---

8. *Idem,* I, 47–8.   9. *Idem,* I, 41.
1. See Thomas Blackwell, *An Enquiry into the Life and Writings of Homer* (London, 1735), p. 2, for a complete statement of the author's purpose. This book is hereafter referred to as Blackwell, *Enquiry.*

and heavenly inspiration.[2] Nor was he convinced that it was really due to an innate poetic skill. Rejecting the contention of many neo-classicists that the two faculties, the judgment and the imagination, were responsible for such works as the *Iliad* and *Odyssey*, Blackwell maintained that Homer's greatness could only be explained in terms of natural or physical causes.[3] In the vein of the modern sociologist, he said that "*young Minds* are apt to receive such strong Impressions from the Circumstances of the Country where they are born and bred, that they contract a mutual kind of *Likeness* to those Circumstances."[4] But Blackwell was not content merely to emphasize the importance of environment in conditioning the mind: he made environment all-important. One's company, education, and experiences in the world all combine to form character, "to make us what we are," as Blackwell expresses it. If this is true for the individual, it must be true for the poet.

The early eighteenth century did not, of course, object to a theory of this sort. What it was less ready to accept was Blackwell's corollary, namely, that no poet could be successful if he strove to be independent of his environment. He says that one "describes nothing so happily, as what he has seen," whether it be a landscape or the customs of a people; and he uses no language so well as his own.[5] To bear out this opinion, Blackwell points to the neoclassic dictum that the "best *Poets* copy from *Nature*," but it is soon clear that he has no neoclassic conception of the term "nature." Instead of demanding an organic unity of parts in a work of art and a generalization of human characters—nature methodized, as Pope says—Blackwell obviously thinks that little more is required than a faithful reproduction of the customs and ideas identified with the age in which the poet lives. He praises *The Way of the World* and *The Rape of the Lock* not because either has any permanent value as literature but because both are true pictures of earlier English society.[6] "The Authors, doubtless, perfectly knew the Life and Manners they were painting, and have succeeded accordingly."[7] At this point a later critic might have insisted upon relativist criticism of Congreve and Pope. Blackwell does not do so. He merely observes that it was the unfortunate lot of

2. *Idem,* p. 3.
3. Blackwell says, "In order to resolve it, you must either ascribe his Superiority to a supernatural divine Assistance, which many of the Ancients firmly believed, tho' *We* do not; or, allowing him to have been an ordinary Man, you must enquire into every *Cause,* natural or accidental, that can possibly have Influence upon the human Mind, towards forming it to Poetry and Verse." Thomas Blackwell (and an unknown continuator), *Letters Concerning Mythology* (London, 1748), p. 37.
4. Blackwell, *Enquiry,* p. 11.   5. *Idem,* p. 29.
6. He asks, "Was there ever a more natural Picture than the *Way of the World?*" *Idem,* p. 34.
7. *Ibid.*

these two poets to have lived at a time when they were obliged to copy from a poor original, a polished and decadent society.

Homer was thus more fortunate than Congreve and Pope. Living in a time when "nature" was more favorable for the creation of poetry, it was possible for him to write a great epic simply by representing "things both in his own and other Countries, *almost as he heard them talked of*,"[8] and above all by depicting men as he found them. Had Homer come into the world earlier, "he could have seen nothing but Nakedness and Barbarity"; had he come later, he would have found the states of Greece lazily enjoying the fruits of peace or carrying on general, well-disciplined struggles against one another.[9] In either case his poetry would have suffered, for it would have been crude on the one hand or it would have lacked passion and simplicity on the other. As it was, he arrived in the interval between the rudeness and extreme orderliness of society,[1] at a moment when arts and learning were in their infancy and passions were still running high.[2] "*Arms* at that time was the honoured Profession, and a publick Spirit the courted Character":[3] one had to fight with determination or there could be no safety "to Life or Fortune." In that age "living by Plunder gave a Reputation for Spirit and Bravery,"[4] and for that reason Homer had no qualms about representing Ulysses as a pirate.[5] Thus, on all sides the Greek poet beheld towns plundered and laid waste, men put to the sword, and women carried off into captivity. He heard the moans of the bereaved, the shrieks of the frightened, and the pleas of the vanquished.

Learning much about mankind under the stress of war—war always reveals the best and worst in men—Homer saw also the beginnings of property and commerce, watching ships arrive from foreign ports with gold and jewels and traders bargain in the market place. He observed the expansion of the Greek communities and the erection of massive walls for protection against marauders. "Nor was it the least instructive Sight, to see a *Colony* led out, a City founded, the Foundations of Order and Policy laid, with all the Provisions for the Security of the People."[6] Thus Homer had the good luck to grow up when he might be a spectator of the various circumstances in which men lived, of their calamities and felicities, of their wars and their mode of life in time of peace.

8. *Idem*, p. 288.   9. *Idem*, p. 35.
1. *Idem*, p. 64.   2. *Idem*, p. 65.   3. *Idem*, p. 53.
4. *Idem*, p. 16. Blackwell says, "These then were the *Manners* in *Homer's* Days; and *such* we find them in his Writings." *Idem*, p. 17.
5. Blackwell says there is no better proof "of the Power that *Manners*, and the *Publick Character* have over Poetry, than the surprising Resemblance of the oldest Writings." Orpheus, Hesiod, and Homer have "the same Epithets of *Gods* and *Men*, the same *Sentiments* and *Allusions*, the same *Cadence* and *Structure*," *Idem*, p. 73.
6. *Idem*, p. 23.

Whatever their occupations might be, Homer's countrymen were simple and open. "The *natural Greek,* in *Homer's* days, covered none of his Sentiments."[7] He told how voraciously he ate, how much he was frightened, and how greatly he enjoyed the pleasures of love and wine;[8] for men had not yet been taught to be ashamed of "their natural Appetites." Living naturally, he and his companions spoke and acted "without other Restraint than their own native Apprehensions of *Good* and *Evil, Just* and *Unjust,* each as he was prompted from *within.*"[9] Not only is a poet better able to imitate such undisguised persons but his representations afford greater pleasure to the reader. Viewing the simplicity of their emotions and their wants, "we begin to love the Men, and wou'd rather have to do with them, than with more refined but *double* Characters."[1]

Thus the nature of men in Homer's age (as distinguished from men in all later ages) was to some extent responsible for the greatness of the *Iliad* and *Odyssey.* To this greatness historical fact also contributed. Instead of attributing the admirable diversity of types of heroes to the poet's skill, as any neoclassicist would do, Blackwell says that in this matter "the Nature and Situation of his Subject bore a considerable Sway."[2] Ever since the Trojan War, the Greeks had considered Ulysses "cautious and bold," Achilles "fierce and impetuous," and Ajax "steady and firm." All that Homer needed to do was to give them the qualities which they were traditionally supposed to have had. As a matter of fact, this was all that he *could* do. It was "Truth and Nature alone that could form those Differences, so real and yet so delicate, and afterwards offer them to a Representation."[3] To describe such a multitude of men "seems to be beyond the Power of Fiction."[4] Thus once again Homer was fortunate—in being able to draw upon events which had actually happened and characters who had actually existed.[5] He was fortunate because those events were great and "full of action" and because so large an assembly of warriors "*must include the prime Characters* of MANKIND."[6]

Another cause of Homer's superiority was the language he used. Again Blackwell thought that the Greek poet had arrived in the world at an opportune moment. Having lost most of its barbarous

7. *Idem,* p. 340. Blackwell says that "the *Grecian's* Wiles are plain and natural: . . . He excels in the simple instructive parts of Life; the Play of the *Passions,* the Prowess of *Bodies,* and those *single Views* of Persons and Characters, that arise from untaught, undisguised Nature." *Idem,* p. 337.

8. *Idem,* p. 340. 9. *Idem,* p. 55. 1. *Idem,* p. 24.

2. *Idem,* pp. 314–15. 3. *Idem,* p. 315. 4. *Ibid.*

5. Blackwell explains that the "Wrath of *Achilles* was in reality the *Hinge of the War.* . . . This made it a kind of *Rule* for the Conduct and Disposition of his Poem: and if he kept it in his Eye (as we see he has certainly done), it would naturally lay out his general *Plan.*" *Idem,* p. 318.

6. *Idem,* p. 312.

character and having progressed at the same pace as society, the language was by that time capable of expressing the best feelings and thoughts of men. It still retained "a sufficient Quantity of its *Original, amazing, metaphoric* Tincture"[7] and a great many quaint phrases and "strong beautiful Expressions"; but there was no enervating refinement to make all poets speak alike in a single "*Set* of courtly Phrases." Blackwell concludes that a language "thoroughly polished in the modern Sense, will not descend to the *Simplicity* of Manners absolutely necessary in *Epic*-Poetry."[8]

As we have seen, a number of earlier critics had discussed the effect of natural surroundings, particularly of climate, upon language and literary works. Nor does Blackwell omit it as one cause of Homer's superiority. Reputedly a native of Asia Minor, the Greek poet had the advantage of dwelling in a land of great fertility, of clear skies, and of incomparable natural beauty, all of which, he says, "*conspire* to bring its Productions of every kind to the highest Perfection." They provided him with a "Mildness of Temper" and a "Flow of Fancy" rarely found in men living in more northerly regions.[9] Besides increasing Homer's poetic powers, this kind of environment provided him with an immense fund of natural images, which he was later to use in the *Iliad* and *Odyssey*.[1]

Turning to the matter of early religion, Blackwell says that "*Homer's Mythology* is but little understood," that modern readers usually consider his fables about the deities "as so many *groundless Fictions*" which the poet could use in any way he wished or even omit if it seemed desirable.[2] Thereupon Blackwell launches into a long disquisition upon the importance of the gods and goddesses. He traces their early origin in Egyptian religious ceremonies and

---

7. *Idem*, p. 47. Blackwell asserts that, in its progress toward perfection, "the *Language* is tinctured in proportion, and bears the Marks of the intermediate Stages." *Idem*, p. 43. In another place Blackwell says that "*Metaphor* is the Produce of all Nations—especially of the Eastern; People given to Taciturnity, of strong Passions, fiery Fancies, and therefore seldom opening their Mouth, but in dark Sayings and mystic Parables. For Metaphor is the Language of *Passion;* as Simile is the Effect of a *warm Imagination*." Blackwell, *Letters Concerning Mythology*, p. 71.

8. Blackwell, *Enquiry*, p. 60. Blackwell says, "Before they are polished into Flattery and refined into Falsehood, we feel the *Force* of their *Words*, and the *Truth* of their *Thoughts*." *Idem*, p. 56.

9. *Idem*, p. 5.

1. Naming countless important poets, philosophers, historians, and physicians, who had come from the same part of the world, Blackwell states that temperate regions give "the best Chance for a fine Perception, and a proportioned Eloquence." *Idem*, p. 6. It must be remembered that the French writer Dubos, in his *Reflexions critiques sur la poesie et sur la peinture*, had done as much as anyone to establish the relation between climatic conditions and the development of the arts. But it would be hard to prove that Blackwell was influenced by the book. He never cites it, referring instead to statements made by Hippocrates and Galen upon this subject.

2. Blackwell, *Enquiry*, p. 148.

shows how and when they were first accepted in Phoenicia, Rhodes, Crete, and finally in Greece. By the time Blackwell draws this extended account to a close, one finds oneself a little bewildered, uncertain just what was to be proved and why it has taken so long to prove it.

There are, however, several facts which Blackwell apparently wanted to impress upon his readers. The first was that Homer accepted rather than invented the religion of his country, employing it in exact accordance with the popular belief. He and Hesiod "wrote from *Life;* and described the Exercise of a Worship long since established in their Country."[3] Because every god had an allegorical meaning, the poet was obliged to use the deities in the proper manner; he could not indifferently place Achilles under the care of Mars, Venus, or Apollo but had to assign him to the god whom he most resembled by nature.[4]

More important was the fact that religion and allegory were at that time *required* in the epic, or, for that matter, in any kind of great poetry. In Homer's day the system derived from Egypt was still new to the Greeks; and philosophers and "speculative incredulous People" had not yet begun to question or ridicule it.[5] Since this religion "was incorporated with their *Manners*," since it had "mixed itself with their Language, and gained *universal Belief*,"[6] Homer could scarcely speak of the manners and actions of men without at the same time speaking of the faith in which they believed.

Still another point made by Blackwell was this: that the poet was *expected* by his audience to narrate fables about the gods. In those days such stories constituted a large part of the marvelous.[7] Simple factual accounts of the origin of the earth, sea, and air had little effect upon the listener. But when the bard "began to unfold the ancient Reign of *hoary Saturn*, the Marvels of the *Golden Age*, and the strange Relation of his *Progeny*," then "the stubborn Multitude opened their Hearts to the wondrous Tale."[8] Furthermore, the Homeric age had no *"Technical* Terms" and "wiredrawn Sciences,"[9]

3. *Idem,* p. 99.
4. According to Blackwell, this was one respect in which Virgil had failed, for he had assigned gods to his heroes without considering whether or not they were properly assigned.
5. *Idem,* p. 148. Blackwell explains that Homer's "Gods and their Powers were never so much as questioned, when he sung of their marvelous Alliances and mystick Generation." *Idem,* p. 287.
6. *Idem,* p. 51.
7. Blackwell says, "For if ever the *Je ne scais quoi* was rightly applied, it is to the *Powers* of Mythology, and the *Faculty* that produces it." *Idem,* p. 157.
8. *Idem,* p. 156.
9. *Idem,* pp. 129–30. Blackwell says that their learning "was wholly *fabulous* and *allegorical.* The Powers of Nature, and Human Passions were the Subject; and they

no abstract knowledge such as men "acquire by Books and Masters."[1]
Because all their learning was contained in allegory, the poet, as the
teacher of men, was supposed to inform his audience at the same
time that he amused it. Had he ignored mythology, abandoning one
source of the marvelous and the only source of instruction, he could
not have been acknowledged a true bard.[2]

What, then, does Blackwell have to say about the nature and occupation of Homer the bard? Was he in any way concerned in the
rise and fall of states and the establishment of laws and religious
beliefs? Our critic seems to consider him more as an observer than
as a man of action, as one who makes it his duty to travel widely,
partly to entertain and partly to discover what was happening in his
day. But Blackwell is not always perfectly consistent. Sometimes he
thinks of Homer as a kind of court poet, who "resorted to the great
Feasts and high Solemnities all over *Greece*, to assist at the Sacrifices,
and entertain the People."[3] Free from *"Care, Business,* or *Want,"*
unawed by laws, and knowing no duties but "those of Hospitality and
Humanity,"[4] he led a life envied by many.[5] Sometimes he thinks of
Homer as a scholar and teacher, learned in philosophy and poetry and
respected by all for his wisdom. And on other occasions Blackwell
assigns Homer the rôle of the rhapsodist, speaking of him as "a blind
stroling Bard"[6] and again as a "'wandering indigent Bard,'"[7] entirely dependent for his subsistence on the good will of his employers.

In giving the Greek poet all these parts to play, Blackwell is apparently making every effort to win respect for Homer's occupation,
to combat the often-mentioned theory that he was only an impecunious balladist. Thus Blackwell states that few people "have conceived
a just Opinion of this Profession, or entered into its Dignity"[8]—
largely because "we have no modern Character like it." Though he

described their various Effects with some Analogy and Resemblance to *Human Actions.' " Idem,* p. 102.

1. *Idem,* pp. 102–03. Technical terms and abstract science, Blackwell claims, "spoil
the natural Faculties, and marr the Expression." *Idem,* p. 130. Referring to some of the
stout defenders of Homer, he says that there is hardly "a depth in *Astronomy,* or latent
Principle in *Heaven* or *Earth,* which they have not discover'd him to be acquainted
with. . . . THESE are indeed very strange Assertions." *Idem,* p. 322.

2. Blackwell's definition of a bard: "A Man who has it in his power to charm our Ears,
entertain our Fancies, and instruct us in the History of our Ancestors; who informs his
wond'ring Audience of the secret Composition, and hidden Harmony of the *Universe,*
of the Order of the *Seasons." Idem,* p. 107.

3. *Idem,* p. 80.   4. *Idem,* p. 116.

5. Blackwell says, "It was indeed no Life of Wealth or Power, but of great *Ease* and
much *Honour." Idem,* p. 114.

6. *Idem,* p. 5.

7. *Idem,* p. 105. Blackwell says, " 'Homer's *being born poor, and living a wandering
indigent Bard, was, in relation to his Poetry, the greatest Happiness that cou'd befall
him.' "* He also calls Homer "a *stroling fanciful Bard." Blackwell, Letters Concerning
Mythology,* p.12.

8. Blackwell, *Enquiry,* p. 113.

sees no similarity between Homer and the *"Irish* or *Highland Rüners,"*[9] he thinks the troubadours of Provence with some justice might be compared to the Greek bard. Thus, too, he rarely uses the term "rhapsodist" when speaking of Homer, a term which had already endangered the reputation of the poet.

But, judging from the critic's description of Homer in action, "rhapsodist" is the term which could best be used.[1] Blackwell refers to him as a singer of "extemporary Strains"[2] and says that while he was "personating a *Hero;* while his Fancy was warming, and his Words flowing; . . . like a Torrent, he wou'd fill up the Hollows of the Work; the boldest Metaphors and glowing Figures wou'd come rushing upon him."[3] Again and again Blackwell urges his readers to put themselves in the place of Homer's audience, to imagine the effect of these stories as they came directly from the mouth of an inspired bard, to realize not only how welcome "miraculous Tales" would be but how easily they could be accepted by a group of hearers whose reason and judgment had been suspended by the magic power of the poet. He was not entertaining the inhabitants of "a *great luxurious City"* but the "martial Race of a wide and free Country, who willingly listen to the Prowess of their Ancestors,"[4] whose passions he knew, whose faces he was constantly studying for reactions. For the first time a Homeric critic was trying to show not merely how the age in general had affected the *Iliad* and *Odyssey* but how the poet had suited these poems to the taste of his audience![5]

This bard or rhapsodist, owing to his profession, saw all of Greece and all kinds of people. He was well acquainted with beggars, warriors, and merchants, and in the courts of great men had an opportunity to become acquainted with the "manner of Conversing and method of Entertaining" among kings and generals; he even learned what kind of "Trinkets their Ladies wore."[6] But the poems also inform us that Homer travelled widely in other countries, particularly in Egypt, where, for the first time, he observed how "every thing was directed by *settled Rules,* and a *digested Policy,"*[7] and where he also gained so much of his information concerning science and theology.

9. *Idem,* p. 114.
1. On one occasion Blackwell says: "nor can the *Strain,* and *Manner* of his Work be felt and relished unless we put ourselves in the place of his Audience, and imagine it coming from the Mouth of a *Rhapsodist." Idem,* p. 122.
2. *Idem,* p. 123.   3. *Idem,* p. 120.
4. *Idem,* p. 123. Blackwell says, "But when we remember his *Profession,* and his common *Audience,* we see the Necessity of *Stories,* and of such as he usually tells." *Idem,* pp. 122–3.
5. Blackwell says, "To this Necessity of pleasing his Audience, I wou'd ascribe that *just Measure* of *Probability and Wonder"* which runs through his poems." *Idem,* p. 121.
6. *Idem,* p. 118. Blackwell notes that Homer mentions "a delicious Pair of *three-stoned Ear-rings."*
7. *Idem,* p. 146.

Blackwell admits that there is no "strict Proof" that Homer visited Egypt but considers it highly probable in view of his minute descriptions of the country—for example, in Achilles' account of the soil, wealth, and policy of Thebes.

As for the region about Troy, Homer certainly knew it well. "*Who* but the Man that had wandered over that delightful Plain, that had viewed the Bendings of the Coast, and every Corner of the Fields, could have described or feigned the genuine *Marks* of it?"[8] According to Blackwell, Homer had the advantage of being the only bard who knew the country of his enemies as well as that of his hero.[9] But he was still more fortunate in having an opportunity to converse with the descendants of the Trojan leaders, to learn what "kind of Men they were; what Armour they wore . . . and how nobly they fought before they fell in Battle."[1]

To us Blackwell's remarks on Homer's knowledge of more distant lands are of greater interest. Some regions in the eastern Mediterranean the poet had undoubtedly visited, since he minutely describes their towns and rivers, their animals and crops, and their arts and sciences.[2] But how was the poet able to speak about the coast of Italy and the cities of Spain? Had he been there too? Because Homer refers to those places in a vague manner, instead of describing them exactly, Blackwell thinks that he heard about them from Phœnician merchants, who made annual voyages into the western Mediterranean and frequently paid calls at Greek ports.[3] Sailors are often inclined to exaggerate their accounts of remote lands, Blackwell says; they imagine, or cause other people to imagine, that strange things happen in a country which has not been thoroughly explored. Hence for Homer the "*Adriatic* Coast, that lies opposite to *Epirus,* and the *Gulph* of *Tarentum,* were too well known, and too much frequented by his Countrymen, to produce many Miracles."[4] But the west coast of Italy was an ideal region from which to derive fabulous stories. There probably were cannibals like the Laestrygonians and, if there

8. *Idem,* p. 293.   9. *Idem,* p. 292.

1. *Idem,* p. 299. Using the information gathered from these people, Homer "has described the Houses of some of the Princes who lived at a great distance from *Troy;* has given us an Inventory of their *Armories,* the Number of *Horses* they kept, and *Chariots* they had laid up,' with all the Circumstances of a *Family Story,* such as might be told by one of their Posterity." *Ibid.*

2. *Idem,* p. 239. Blackwell explains that Homer described the coast around the entire Mediterranean Sea: "but with this difference, that he speaks of the *North-East* End of it, so particularly and minutely, as to convince his Reader, that he had visited it *in Person.*"

3. Blackwell says that "*Homer* was more capable of giving than receiving Instruction in the *Geography* of *Greece, the Lesser Asia,* and perhaps the *Egyptian Coast:* But what further Knowledge appears in his Writings of the other Tracts of Land in *Europe, Asia,* and *Africa, That,* I judge, he has received by Information from the *Phenicians.*" *Idem,* p. 236.

4. *Idem,* p. 246.

were no sirens exactly as Homer describes them, travellers at least found lewd women who lured them ashore and tried to prevent them from returning to their ships.[5] Even Scylla and Charybdis were only two dangerous rocks between which it was sometimes necessary to pass. In stormy weather it would be easy to imagine that they were creatures eager to destroy the ships and men. Blackwell concludes that, "how wild and fabulous soever" such tales may appear, "there are few of them, but upon enquiry, we find to have some natural Foundation."[6]

Summing up the argument of his book, Blackwell says that Homer became the father of poetry and the greatest poet the world has ever known by "the *united* Influence of the happiest CLIMATE, the most natural MANNERS, the boldest LANGUAGE, and most expressive RELIGION: When *these* were applied to so rich a Subject as the War between Greece and Troy, they produced the ILIAD and ODYS-SEY."[7] It is no wonder, he decides, that two poems such as these should appear only once in three or four thousand years, considering how many "rare CHANCES" and "uncommon INGREDIENTS" had combined to make them excel.[8]

In some respects it is possible to associate Blackwell with the Ancients fifteen or twenty years earlier. He has their unbounded enthusiasm for the literature of the classical world and their distaste for anything modern. He also views Homeric society as ideal and that of recent times as degenerate. He has the same tendency to use absolute standards in criticizing, to begin with an assumption—in his case, that Homer has never been equalled or surpassed—and then use history to prove the justice of his assumption. It must be remembered, however, that absolute standards are not confined to literary criticism at the beginning of the century, that the primitivists after 1750 turned to the historical approach to support their prejudice in favor of Ossian. In fact, Blackwell's criticism is fundamentally akin to that of the later Scotch writers, foreshadowing their historical points of view rather than summarizing the theories and methods of Mme. Dacier and her followers. For example, instead of venturing occasionally and briefly into historical speculation from the safe confines of neoclassicism, as so many of his predecessors had done, Blackwell cuts off all possibility of retreat in professing a thoroughly historical approach. He makes it obvious that he is straddling no fence. He does not at one time claim that that poetry is good which is basically timeless and at another that the creation of great poetry was

5. Blackwell says " 'they were *leud Women,* who prostituted themselves to the Sailors, and, by the Allurements of a lazy voluptuous Life, made them unmindful of their Voyage, and careless of returning to their native Country.' " *Idem,* p. 259.
6. *Idem,* pp. 247–8.   7. *Idem,* p. 345.   8. *Idem,* pp. 345–6.

made possible by an environment which existed for a moment and cannot exist again. For him, as for the primitivist, each poem is highly individual, having its own place in time; it is fundamentally rather than superficially different from every other poem. This is so because of forces over which the poet himself has little if any control. His own unique experiences, the welter of ideals, manners, and superstitions of his age, all that the poet has seen or heard—these, as Blackwell says, "produce" the poem. In fact, so firmly is the poet bound by environment that only two means of escape are possible. He can, if he wishes, become an ignoble imitator of other poets or he may write of bygone times of which he knows next to nothing.

Nor is Blackwell's conception of Homer the poet at all similar to that of the early eighteenth-century writers, almost all of whom, Ancients and Moderns alike, had continued to think of Homer as a conscious, skilled creator. It is true, of course, that this traditional view had begun to lose ground during the height of the Battle. Use of history had prompted suggestions that Homer had been a balladist and writer of romances, and ever-closer association of the poet with his age (a barbarous age), as well as revived interest in biography, had given added encouragement to those suggestions. Blackwell, however, took the final step. For him the age did not merely "affect" the poet; it "formed" him, so to speak. If refined and polished, like the present age, it produced such refined and polished artists as Congreve and Pope. If rude and unsophisticated, like Homer's, the greatest exertion of genius could not prevent its poets from being rude and unsophisticated. It was therefore necessary to draw a new picture of Homer. Homer became like other men of his time, sharing their outlook on life, their beliefs and ideals. As a poet, he became the wandering mendicant, the singer and observer, rather than the all-knowing "rational" artist—the inspired rhapsodist telling of things that were fact and fiction, of things he had seen or heard but never of things he himself had invented. In short, Blackwell formed a view of Homer which was almost the opposite of the old one. It was a view that was never to be forgotten. It was to be accepted by the Scotch and later by the Germans.

Blackwell's estimate of Greek society was also new. As we have seen, critics in the time of Mme. Dacier had invariably gone to one extreme or the other, some thinking of Greek life in terms of simple habits and gentle virtues, others in terms of violence and childish impetuosity. While a few critics were aware that the Greeks at peace were very different from the Greeks at war, no effort had been made to form a complete picture of Homeric society. Nor did the most fanatic of the Ancients find the least good in the brutality of Homer's heroes. It was an important step, therefore, when Blackwell united the seemingly opposed characteristics of the Homeric age. For him the Greeks were primitive—neither barbaric nor refined. Their spontaneity and their animalistic passions, to which so many objections had been raised by critics of every stripe, balanced their "domestic" virtues and produced a more interesting and varied national character than that of any people before or since. One could therefore find some good in every quality of the early Greek. He could, and Blackwell did, idealize Greek life as described by Homer. But Blackwell goes still further. He shows, while the Ancients had only intimated, that the very nature of a poem is largely determined by the nature of the society in which it is written. Greek society happened to favor the creation of great epics, for it was varied and interesting, making it possible for the poet to copy the "prime characters of mankind." As Blackwell says, a certain set of circumstances "produced" the *Iliad* and *Odyssey*.

In yet another way the *Enquiry* seems to foreshadow later criticism. The book suggests, though it does not consider, a question which mid-eighteenth-century critics were to try to answer. The question is this: why has no other society, in its progress toward refinement, produced a Homer? For instance, why is it that Anglo-Saxon society did not "form" an epic poet different from but equal to Homer? Apparently Blackwell thinks of the development of society as a process covering thousands of years, beginning in Greece, continuing in Rome, and reaching an undesirable state of refinement in western Europe. That separate nations or peoples may go through this evolution, reaching a point similar to that of the Homeric Greeks and producing poets more or less like Homer, was a theory that was to arise only with more thorough study of primitive peoples. Nor did Blackwell or his followers satisfactorily settle another point which their criticism raises. No effort was made to determine to what extent the poet is dependent upon his own abilities. If environment is the real maker of poets, why was Homer the only outstanding poet of his time? Blackwell, of course, mentions that Homer was an acute observer and assumes that he had special talents for expression. But on the whole he studiously avoids talking about the mental gifts of the poet, as if they were of no great importance. He will not even apply the term "genius" to Homer.

Also similar to those of the later critics are Blackwell's occasional inconsistencies. To take an example, Blackwell usually says that to be ideally primitive both society and poetry require a combination of spontaneity and restraint. On other occasions, however, he seems to emphasize only the importance of spontaneity. The Greek warrior in battle, in his eating and drinking, and the poet in describing the deeds of gods and men are praised because they do not hold themselves back in the least. As Blackwell says, they are "natural"; they give free rein to their emotions. In the same way, the later Scotch critics, when dealing with Ossian alone, associate the primitive with complete lack of restraint, with unhampered self-expression. However, the term "primitive" is often applied to a society or literature which is neither barbaric nor refined. Ossian then becomes their ideal as a primitive poet and Homer becomes the best example of the barbaric poet. In fact, as we shall see, there is scarcely a single Scotch critic who does not object in the strongest language to the reckless manner in which Homer's characters eat and drink, kill and torture—who does not think of Ossian, particularly in his "sentiments," as the more refined of the two poets. It would seem, therefore, that later Scotch criticism was at least based upon that of Blackwell. Blackwell did not convince them as to the superiority of Homer but his estimates of the primitive poet and the ideal society had a marked effect upon their literary theories.

IV

Scotch Criticism after 1750

LITERARY criticism in England, after the middle of the eighteenth century, was rapidly becoming less aesthetic and more historical. While many critics continued to emphasize the formal and timeless aspects of works of art, a new period of criticism was being established by other critics and scholars more conscious of the principle of change and growth, a principle which appeared to them to operate in the field of literature as much as in political and social history. Interest shifted, more and more, from the universal qualities of art to the special circumstances under which works had been composed. Some critics, such as Edward Young and Joseph Warton, laid stress upon the uniqueness of the education, the career, and the mental qualities of the poet himself. Others, taking a broader view, endeavored to reconstruct medieval and Renaissance society and to arrive at a better understanding of literary works by showing how the time of writing largely determined the thing written. Among this latter group were such critics as Elizabeth Montagu and Richard Hurd, who, in idealizing early English poetry, helped prepare the way for the romantic criticism of authors like Chaucer, Spenser, and Shakespeare.

In Scotland the same development occurred. Perhaps the tendency to turn to the historical approach was even plainer in a group of primitivists including Hugh Blair, Henry Home, Adam Ferguson, and James Macpherson.[1] Sharing a keen interest in the relation of literature to society, an interest heightened by the discovery of Ossian and the subsequent controversy over Ossianic origins, these men published disquisitions on primitive Highland poetry that have been rightly recognized as a means by which romantic criticism came into vogue.

But little attention has been paid to their analyses of Ossian's great rival, Homer, his relation to Ossian, and the rôle which Scotch comments on Homer played in literary criticism thirty or forty years later. It was natural that the interest in cultural history and early poetry should lead these writers to speak of the Greek poet and that they should compare him both explicitly and implicitly to Ossian.

1. The most complete and authoritative study of the historical points of view of Scotch and English critics of the eighteenth century is René Wellek's *Rise of English Literary History* (Chapel Hill, 1941).

Equally natural was the kind of Homeric criticism which emerged from these comparisons. Basing their appraisals almost entirely upon the content of carefully selected passages of each poet, the patriotic Scotch characterized Ossian as refined and moral, while Homer for the first time appeared impassioned, crude, and barbaric, of small value to anyone except the historian. Their opinions of Homer and the parallels between Homer and Ossian help to account for the introduction of historical criticism and the rise of romantic Hellenism somewhat later on.

As it was suggested earlier, Thomas Blackwell was a prominent figure in forming primitivist literary theory in Scotland. The *Enquiry* was well known and so was Blackwell himself. Appointed professor of Greek at Marischal College, Aberdeen, in 1725,[2] Blackwell taught until his death in 1757. Over this long period of time, one of his main objects, if we may believe his biographers and his students, was to revive interest in ancient culture.[3] Speaking of the new "taste for polite literature" which had sprung up in Scotland in the second and third quarters of the century, John Ramsay says that "the first essays were made in the Marischal College by a man of very singular character. Dr. Thomas Blackwell . . . was an elegant and enthusiastic classical scholar, and withal a man of a vigorous mind, improved by erudition."[4] He applauds the professor for "lending a helping hand to raise a poor neglected college to high repute."[5] Though not particularly popular among his associates, who disliked his affectation and "Bentleian arrogance," Blackwell appears to have inspired a large number of the students working under him. Ramsay says that "some of them . . . continued as long as they lived to believe that he had fed them with hidden manna,"[6] and Alexander Gerard has the highest praise for his ability as a teacher. "No man ever possessed in a more eminent degree the talent of inspiring young minds with a love of learning; of begetting among them a generous emulation; and of forming them to a taste and perception of what was elegant and beautiful in the admired productions of antiquity."[7] According to Robert Chambers, Gerard, George Campbell, and James Beattie were in Blackwell's class;[8] and it is probably safe to say that William

2. Some works place the date as early as 1723.

3. A summary of Blackwell's activities as professor of Greek may be found in Lois Whitney's article, "English Primitivistic Theories of Epic Origins," *Modern Philology*, XXI (May, 1924), 337–78.

4. John Ramsay, *Scotland and Scotsmen in the Eighteenth Century*, Alexander Allardyce, ed. (Edinburgh and London, 1888), I, 291.

5. *Idem*, I, 293.   6. *Idem*, I, 292.

7. Alexander Gerard, "A Character of Dr. Thomas Blackwell," in A. F. Tytler, *Memoirs of the Life and Writings of the Honourable Henry Home of Kames* (Edinburgh, 1814), III, 74.

8. Robert Chambers, *A Biographical Dictionary of Eminent Scotsmen* (Glasgow, 1835), I, 237. Chambers says, "He had the merit of rearing some very eminent Greek

Duff, John Ogilvie, and James Macpherson, all Marischal men who later won their spurs in the literary world, were at least acquainted with the author of the *Enquiry* during their student days.[10] Nor should one forget James Burnet, later Lord Monboddo.[1] Chambers says that he was one of Blackwell's "greatest admirers, and [most] zealous imitators in the prosecution of Grecian learning";[2] and Ramsay states that he seemed "to have taken his passion for Greek" from the professor.[3]

It would seem probable that Blackwell's success as a teacher was partly responsible for the adoption of many of his ideas by this group of Scotch critics. But the *Enquiry* itself, which was still a comparatively recent book when these men came to Aberdeen, was by no means unknown.[4] Gerard says that the work enabled Blackwell to acquire "at once that distinguished character in the learned world, which he ever supported with so much credit and reputation."[5] James Beattie, in his essay "Of Memory and Imagination," states that the "very learned writer of an inquiry into the life and writings of Homer has proved, or at least made it highly probable, that the great father of poetry himself was . . . indebted for the transcendency of his genius, to the manners of his age."[6] As we shall see, both Beattie and Blair went to the *Enquiry* for some of their ideas about Homer. John Ogilvie, in dealing with ancient religion, refers to Blackwell as a "learned modern writer" and quotes from the *Enquiry* in support of one of his arguments.[7] Lord Kames not only speaks of the professor's book but devotes several pages of his *Sketches of the History of Man* to a consideration of some of the historical problems raised by Blackwell.[8] Finally, John Brown, while not always agreeing with the *Enquiry*, cites this work several times in his study of the origin of poetry.[9]

It would be assuming too much to say that this group of men, several of them primitivists, drew their principal ideas about early society from Blackwell. Nevertheless, they, like Blackwell, were pri-

scholars, among whom may be mentioned Principal George Campbell, Dr Alexander Gerard, and Dr James Beattie."

10. Blackwell taught the introductory course in Greek. Chambers says that he was "a very general subject of conversation" in the college. *Idem*, I, 239.

1. Monboddo, however, rarely speaks about Homer.

2. *Idem*, I, 424.   3. Ramsay, *Scotland and Scotsmen*, I, 351.

4. Tytler speaks of Blackwell's book as "instructive, both from the just criticism, and the variety of classical matter which it contains." Tytler, *op. cit.*, I, 231.

5. *Idem*, III, 73.

6. *The Works of James Beattie* (Philadelphia, 1809), I, 230.

7. John Ogilvie, *Philosophical and Critical Observations on the Nature, Characters, and Various Species of Composition* (London, 1774), I, 414–15, n.

8. Henry Home, Lord Kames, *Sketches of the History of Man* (Edinburgh, 1778), I, 275–8.

9. John Brown, *A Dissertation on the Rise, Union, and Power, the Progressions, Separations, and Corruptions, of Poetry and Music* (London, 1763), pp. 81, 98–9, 154.

marily interested in the more remote periods of history and in the beginnings of literature. Like him, these critics used the historical approach almost entirely, trying to discover under what conditions poetry first came into existence rather than prescribing how the bard should have written.[1] Again like him, they brought together historical facts and such evidence as poetry itself could afford, in an endeavor to bring to light the peculiar circumstances affecting poetic creation at any given time and in any given country. Finally, the majority of these writers followed Blackwell in characterizing the heroic age as very early and nearly barbaric, at the same time that they respected, if not all its qualities, at least its simplicity, frankness, and passion. Considering Blackwell's prominent academic position and the occasional citations of the *Enquiry* by the Scotch critics, it would appear probable that he did contribute something to their conceptions of primitive society and in several cases to their estimate of Homer and the Homeric period.[2]

Most of the Scotch critics of Homer and Ossian believed that a society and its literature could hardly be considered apart, that one's knowledge of an early period was often to be gained by a study of its poetry, and, in turn, that one's estimate of early poetry was to be based on a study of the period to which it belonged. In effect, such a close association of poet and age led to two implications. In the first place, it meant that there was to be no logical distinction between social historian and literary critic, that a writer who examined and criticized society as represented in the *Iliad* was entitled, at the same time, to judge Homer the poet by historical rather than purely artistic standards.[3] Hence one finds among the Scotch writers that every illustration of barbaric manners among Homeric characters contributed to the theory that Homer himself was little more than a barbarian. In the second place, the close relation of poet and age meant something even more directly important to the study of the develop-

---

1. It was perhaps owing to this desire to find out how Homer had written, to view him as his own age viewed him, that led to a general rebellion by the Scotch against Pope's translations of Homer. For example, in his "Remarks on the Utility of Classical Learning," James Beattie said that Homer's simplicity, impetuosity, and "majestick inattention to the more trivial niceties of style" cannot be found in the English version. Beattie, *op. cit.*, VI, 374. Brown discovered that Pope has included "fine *moral* Traits" which are absent in Homer, and that Pope has abandoned "the native and unpolished Simplicity" for which the Greek bard is so highly prized. Brown, *op. cit.*, p. 82. Lord Kames censured the English translator because he had not given a true picture of Homeric manners. Pope, he stated, considered it below the dignity of Achilles "to act the butcher," forgetting that one of our greatest pleasures in reading Homer arises from the "lively picture of ancient manners" which the poet draws. Kames, *op. cit.*, I, 336, n.

2. There is no way of *proving* how great Blackwell's influence was. One can only say that writers seem to have had the *Enquiry* in mind far more often than they actually quoted from it or referred to it.

3. In the case of some of the Scotch writers, it is often difficult, in fact, to decide whether their interests are primarily historical or literary.

ment of the historical approach, namely, that for the first time neo-classic principles were being almost entirely rejected by large numbers of critics. For them the value of Homer's poetry lay in its content: in its faithful representation of the ideas, customs, morals, and manners of a people of a distant age. That there was any excellence in Homer which was timeless and, one might say, nonhistorical does not seem to have occurred to many of these critics.

Perhaps nothing indicates the time-consciousness of the Scotch critics more clearly than their agreement that great difficulties face those who would apply the historical approach to Homer. Commenting on the impossibility of adopting the Greek point of view, David Hume states that any critic who attempted to discover why "such a particular poet, as HOMER . . . existed, at such a place, in such a time, would throw himself headlong into chimaera."[4] Similarly, Alexander Gerard says that the "refinement to which we are accustomed in modern times, renders the simplicity of manners which Homer attributes to his heroes, an object of surprise."[5] Indeed, so sharply are the "polite" and the "low" distinguished in modern times that "we must put a sort of force upon our minds" in order to separate those elements of ancient manners which were accounted simple from those which were accounted "mean" in Homer's day. Another critic, Hugh Blair, warns the Homeric student that one "is not to look for the correctness, and elegance, of the Augustan Age" in the *Iliad* and *Odyssey*. Instead, he is to expect a "picture of the antient world." "He must reckon upon finding characters and manners, that retain a considerable tincture of the savage state; moral ideas, as yet, imperfectly formed; and the appetites and passions of men brought under none of those restraints, to which, in a more advanced state of Society, they are accustomed."[6] In other words, a critic who uses the historical approach should not assume, as the neoclassicist had done, that Homer was a conscious artist, a skilled master whose poems are largely timeless creations. Knowing him to be an early poet, the student and reader should realize that the *Iliad* and *Odyssey* are necessarily representative of a certain period in the development of society and are indelibly marked by that period; that, as John Brown suggests, Homer "painted what he saw, and believed, and painted truly."[7]

4. *Essays Moral, Political and Literary by David Hume*, T. H. Green and T. H. Grose, eds. (London, 1875), I, 177. Hume was probably thinking of Blackwell's statement that "natural causes" produced the *Iliad* and *Odyssey*.

5. Alexander Gerard, *An Essay on Genius* (London, 1774), p. 103.

6. Hugh Blair, *Lectures on Rhetoric and Belles Lettres* (London, 1787), III, 231-2.

7. Brown, *op. cit.*, p. 82. None of the Scotch critics seem to have regarded Homer as an inventor. Wilkie, who believed epic poetry should be founded on popular traditions, says, "I could even as soon be persuaded that all that Homer has written is strict matter of fact, as believe that any one mortal man was capable of inventing that infinite variety

Realizations of this kind led inevitably to detailed discussions of the society which the Greek poet had portrayed so faithfully. Perhaps because he did not wholly sympathize with the ideas of other Scotch writers, James Beattie had no definite conception of Homeric society. If the Greeks had only begun to emerge from the savage state and were no more advanced than the neighboring tribes, how can one explain the perfection which their language had attained when Homer wrote? Likewise, how can one account for the poet's descriptions of the magnificence of Trojan palaces? Beattie foresaw that some critics would reply to the latter question by calling attention to the servile occupations of persons dwelling in those palaces. Consequently he sought an explanation of the behavior of kings and princesses in the peculiar circumstances of the times. Though it was no more barbaric than in the age of Ossian, "society was more unsettled than it is now." Rulers might be wealthy and might even live in great ease but they were subject to sudden changes of fortune and were as liable "to cold, weariness, and hunger, as the meanest of their people."[8] Necessity, and necessity alone, obliged them to be adventurous and obliged them to become acquainted with all the "arts of life."[9]

Essentially the same was Adam Ferguson's estimate of Homeric society.[1] When the Greek poet arrived in the world, men were living in a "rude and infant state"[2] but were no longer grouped together in tribes in which one individual was virtually as important as another. Simultaneously with the formation of communities, property had come into existence and with it the separation of society into ranks. This separation was not very clearly defined, however, for leader and follower often slept together on the ground and ate from the same dish. The children of the king and those of the subject tended the flocks, and even the "keeper of the swine was a prime counsellor at the court of Ulysses."[3] At the same time, in a society of this kind men still preserve "many parts of their earliest character." "They are still adverse to labour, addicted to war, admirers of fortitude, and, in the language of Tacitus, more lavish of their blood than of their sweat."[4] Because of the hope of spoil and honor, the hero of the *Iliad* "takes every advantage of an enemy, to kill with safety to himself" and

---

of historical circumstances which occur in the works of that celebrated poet; for invention is by no means an easy thing." William Wilkie, *The Epigoniad* (Edinburgh, 1757), p. xxxvii.

8. Beattie's views on Homeric language may be found in William Forbes, *An Account of the Life and Writings of James Beattie* (New York, 1807), p. 169.

9. Beattie, *op. cit.*, v, 202–03.

1. Ferguson was primarily a historian. His views on Homeric society are important, however, since they have a direct bearing on his literary criticism.

2. Adam Ferguson, *An Essay on the History of Civil Society* (Edinburgh, 1767), p. 113.

3. *Idem*, p. 153.   4. *Idem*, p. 149.

rarely feels any commiseration for those whom he has conquered.[5] Because of the inequalities among ranks of society, domestic disorders are frequent; men fight one another, take vengeance upon their neighbors, and in general become "hunters of Men."[6] Such a society, Ferguson realizes, seems barbaric indeed. But he hastens to point out that war and the love of spoil, while making the Greek a terrible opponent, had the salutary effect of knitting the bonds of friendship closer than ever.[7] In other words, some of those traits which the Moderns unhesitatingly brand as vicious served to bring out the nobler qualities of men. Ferguson sums up this part of his argument with the remark that "Homer either lived with a people in this stage of their progress, or found himself engaged to exhibit their character."[8] To us the remark is particularly significant, since it suggests either the complete association of the poet with his age or, in agreement with other critics of the day, the possibility that the poet had no choice other than that of representing men *exactly* as they had been at an earlier time.[9]

With such critics as Blair and Macpherson, Lord Kames shared a deep passion for Ossianic society. He did not see "how it is credible, that a people, rude at present and illiterate, were, in the infancy of their society, highly refined in sentiment and manners," but at the same time he vigorously upheld the authenticity of the Highland poems and ranked Ossian among the great epic poets of the world. In fact, it was undoubtedly this enthusiasm for Ossian which led him, of all the Scotch critics, to adopt the least sympathetic attitude toward Homer and Homeric society. He declared that there was little difference between the followers of Achilles and their brutal neighbors. They were "like other savages," he says at one time;[1] on another occasion he observes that "no savages are more cruel than the Greeks and Trojans were, as described by Homer."[2] Not only did they kill in cold blood, reduce towns to ashes, and disregard the sex and age of their victims but they retained enough "of the savage character, as, even without blushing, to fly from an enemy superior in bodily strength."[3] Kames is rather surprised to find that Homer could describe the arts and regal magnificence of the Phaeacians "with the same breath" that he portrayed the daughter of Alcinous riding to the river "on a waggon of greasy cloaths." The Greeks, he assures us,

5. *Idem*, p. 307.　　　　　　6. *Idem*, p. 150.
7. *Idem*, p. 154.　　　　　　8. *Idem*, p. 148.
9. Ferguson observes that we would be disgusted by the narrations of the actions of early man if writers did not, "like Homer . . . make us forget the horrors of a vindictive, cruel, and remorseless proceeding towards an enemy, in behalf of the strenuous conduct, the courage, and vehement affections, with which the hero maintained the cause of his friend and of his country." *Idem*, p. 298. In all probability, such a statement would not have been made by any critic at the beginning of the century.
1. Kames, *op. cit.*, I, 169.　　2. *Idem*, I, 348.　　　　3. *Idem*, I, 351-2.

considered the action of Nausicaa wholly commendable, but this only proves that they "were not sensible of the lowness of their manners."[4] Judging from these remarks and from his observation that the Greek heroes had no spoons, forks, tablecloths, and napkins, we might be led to suppose that Kames had little sympathy for the Homeric age and consequently for the descriptions of that society in the *Iliad* and *Odyssey*.[5] On other occasions, however, he seems to respect the "natural" way of life among the Greeks. It is the "lively picture of ancient manners," he says, which gives us "one of the capital pleasures . . . in perusing Homer."[6]

John Brown also considered the Homeric poems representative of a primitive society. In them, he says, "we find the *Religion, Polities,* and *Manners* of ancient GREECE displayed with all the Appearances of Truth, because delivered with all their Imperfections." Strength, courage, and cunning are ever the ruling virtues during "the rude Progress of barbarous Manners"; and because every man in that age admires them the poet assigns these virtues to both men and gods. Hence, while Homer is the "supreme Painter of natural Manners," one cannot consider either his ideas or the ideas of his contemporaries sufficiently advanced to embrace "those abstract general Principles of moral Excellence or Blame."[7] Brown was not only completely at odds with Le Bossu and the vast majority of neoclassic critics since the Renaissance—most of whom justified the *Iliad* and *Odyssey* on the ground that they afforded admirable instruction in morality—but he even took issue with an important critic who used a historical approach, Thomas Blackwell. Quoting a passage from the *Enquiry*, in which Homer's capability as a moral teacher had been defended, Brown asks, "Where is *Virtue* praised? Is it in the Conduct of the natural *Greek*, who looked upon *no means* as *base* to escape Danger? . . . Is it in the Conduct of AGAMEMNON, who declared his *Passion* for a *Captive*, and his *Neglect* of his *Queen*, in the *Face* of the *whole Army?*"[8] Apparently Blackwell's interpretation of Homer's "moral lessons" was not "historical" enough to satisfy Brown!

4. *Idem*, 1, 381–2.

5. Kames observes that the nations engaged in the Trojan War had only advanced from the "shepherd" to the "agricultural" state. He says that "Homer lived in a rude age, little advanced in useful arts, and still less in civilization and enlarged benevolence." *Idem*, 1, 276.

6. *Idem*, 1, 336. In judging the merit of the Homeric poems, it would appear that Kames usually favored the application of neoclassic principles. However much Homer was affected by his environment, Kames was inclined to regard the Greek poet as a "blazing star" in a barbarous age. See *idem*, 1, 281.

7. Brown, *op. cit.*, pp. 78–9. Brown says that, while "HOMER was a compleat *natural Painter* of the Ways of Men," he was at the same time "an imperfect moral Painter from the *unpolished* Genius and *barbarous Legislation* of the Age in which he lived." *Idem*, p. 80.

8. *Idem*, p. 81.

David Hume substantially agreed with Brown that the "ethics of Homer" were rather crude. "We are displeased to find the limits of vice and virtue so confounded," he declares,[9] and to some extent this fault impairs the value of the *Iliad* and *Odyssey* so far as the modern reader is concerned. However, Hume's approach to poetry was historical enough to permit him to say that, much as the moderns may disapprove of Homer's sentiments, the realization that "ideas of morality and decency" alter from age to age obliges one to exonerate the poet himself.[1] In all "uncultivated nations" which have not discovered the merit of "beneficence" and "justice," courage is recognized as the greatest excellence,[2] even as "bodily strength and dexterity" are certain to receive more emphasis than they do among men nowadays[3]—simply because they are more useful and important in the warlike kind of existence led by primitive people.

Though it was commonly believed in the eighteenth century that peace and the advancement of all the arts were required for the production of great literature, the Scotch writers hastened to point out that the success of the *Iliad* and *Odyssey* depended largely upon Homer's having lived during or shortly after a period of political turmoil and military activity. Thus Beattie declared, perhaps thinking of Blackwell, that the "wars of Thebes and Troy are undoubtedly to be reckoned among the causes that gave rise to the literature of Greece";[4] and Lord Kames, while maintaining that Homer's genius was the true explanation of his superiority, stated that an "important action of doubtful event" is often responsible for the creation of great poetry.[5]

None of the critics explains in detail the manner in which primitive warfare might have encouraged Homer to compose the *Iliad* and *Odyssey* or how military expeditions and civil uprisings could have affected the nature of those poems. Instead, they preferred to deal with the character of the early Greeks. They chose to revive the theory emphasized so strongly by Blackwell: that Homer had the best possible materials with which to work. In one of his essays Blair says that "antient manners, how much soever they contradict our present notions of dignity and refinement, afford, nevertheless, materials for Poetry, superior, in some respects, to those which are furnished by a more polished state of Society." Human nature is more open and undisguised, "free scope" is given "to the strongest and most impetuous emotions of the mind," and the prejudices and appetites of men are all laid bare. Together with a strength and boldness of style,

9. Green and Grose, *op. cit.*, I, 283.   1. *Idem*, I, 282.
2. David Hume, *Enquiries Concerning the Human Understanding and the Principles of Morals*, L. A. Selby-Bigge, ed. (Oxford, 1902), p. 255.
3. *Idem*, p. 245.   4. Beattie, *op. cit.*, III, 76.
5. Kames, *op. cit.*, I, 190–1.

ancient Greek manners are responsible for "the two great characters of the Homeric Poetry": fire and simplicity.[6] With Blair both Brown[7] and Duff agreed, Duff in particular emphasizing the "SIMPLICITY and UNIFORMITY of ancient Manners" in contrast to the refinement of modern manners.[8]

In Beattie's treatment of the subject, the hand of Blackwell is evident. He says that there is one period in history in which the manners of men offer the best subject for poetical creation: "I mean, that wherein men are raised above savage life, and considerably improved by arts, government, and conversation; but not advanced so high in the ascent towards politeness, as to have acquired a habit of disguising their thoughts and passions, and of reducing their behaviour to the uniformity of the mode." This was the age in which Homer "had the good fortune" to live. Now, it is true that the manners of Achilles and Sarpedon do belong to a specific period. But, owing to the fact that these heroes have passions "unperverted by luxury," "powers unenervated by effeminacy," and "thoughts disengaged from artificial restraint," their characters "approach to the nature of poetical or general ideas" and hence please all ages.[9] Beattie concludes that the simple manners of Homer's warriors "may disgust a Terrasson, or a Chesterfield" but will always please "the universal taste."[1] A similar view is taken by Pinkerton. He speaks of the Homeric age as a time when "the sun of science is beginning to rise" but men still give rein to their passions.[2] Such an environment produced a "warmth" and "rapidity" in Homer's poetry.

Also conducive to Homer's success as a poet was the kind of religion which obtained among these belligerent, spontaneous Greeks. Duff says that "it was certainly a peculiar felicity" for Homer "to have found a theological system, already invented and in repute, so admirably adapted to his design." He was able to make the gods interested in the fate of individual warriors, to assign them parts to play in directing the events of the Trojan War, and in general to increase the "grandeur and dignity of his action" by having them mingle with his human characters.[3] With Duff, John Ogilvie agreed. The Christian religion, he said, was ill-adapted to epic poetry. But ancient mythology afforded great advantages to the early bard and "Homer appears to have availed himself of all the benefits derived

---

6. Blair, op. cit., III, 234.   7. See Brown, op. cit., p. 26.
8. William Duff, An Essay on Original Genius and Its Various Modes of Exertion in Philosophy and the Fine Arts, Particularly in Poetry (London, 1767), p. 290.
9. Beattie, op. cit., v, 224–5. Beattie says, "This was the period at which the manners of men are most picturesque, and their adventures most romantick."
1. Idem, v, 227.
2. Robert Heron (John Pinkerton), Letters of Literature (London, 1785), p. 6.
3. William Duff, Critical Observations on the Writings of the Most Celebrated Original Geniuses in Poetry (London, 1770), p. 191.

from the religion of his country." For example, it was possible for him to combine divine qualities and human frailties in the characters of his gods and thus to paint some of the most "entertaining personages of his fable." He could alter the traditional accounts of the deities to suit his own purposes because this was a practice commonly followed by poets at that time.[4]

Finally, the critics with whom we have been concerned had a conception of Homer himself altogether different from that of the neoclassicists. Their idea often approached that of Blackwell, who pictured the Greek poet as a spontaneous bard, stirred by the tremendous activity of early Greek life, viewing on the one hand the beginnings of art and on the other the rise and fall of cities. As a matter of fact, in the course of his study of primitive poetry, John Brown quotes several passages from the *Enquiry* dealing with the origin of the bard; and on one occasion he says that "a late learned Author hath, in many Circumstances, though not in all, given a just Idea" of the "*Profession* and *Art*" of the ancient poet.[5] Brown was, of course, more concerned with showing why and under what conditions poetry arose than with discussing the manner in which the *Iliad* and *Odyssey* were composed. It is therefore difficult to say whether or not he agreed with Blackwell that Homer was a kind of rhapsodist. While he acknowledges that "HOMER followed the honourable Profession of a *Bard*, and sung his own Poems at the public Feasts,"[6] he ordinarily associates the term "enthusiasm" with the songs of earlier poets, with the less artistic hymns and odes of the primitive singer. Because of his emphasis upon the "Epic PLAN" of the *Iliad*, a plan "so *complex*, so *vast*, and yet so *perfect*,"[7] one is inclined to believe that Brown considered Homer something of a conscious artist or at least one of the very last of the early inspired bards.

James Beattie, on the other hand, followed faithfully in the footsteps of his master, Thomas Blackwell. He speaks of Homer's "simplicity," his "impetuosity," and his "majestick inattention to the more trivial niceties of style." Supporting the statement with a long quotation from the *Enquiry*, Beattie declares that "Homer in Greek seems to sing extempore, and from immediate inspiration, or enthusiasm."[8] He does not go on to say that Homer the rhapsodist knew nothing of the art of writing but he does suggest that the bard "composed his immortal work at a time when writing was not common; when people were rather hearers than readers of poetry."[9] Beattie also observes that Homer had endured poverty and weariness throughout

4. Ogilvie, *op. cit.*, I, 332–3.   5. Brown, *op. cit.*, pp. 98–9.
6. *Idem*, p. 105. Again referring to Blackwell, Brown says "He represents them [the bards] as wandering Musicians only, who were *welcome* to the Houses of the *Great*. Such indeed they were, in the *later* Periods." *Idem*, p. 99.
7. *Idem*, p. 104.   8. Beattie, *op. cit.*, VI, 374.   9. *Idem*, V, 263, n.

his adventuresome life, that he had often been dependent upon "the meanest" and was not denied the society of the greatest.[1] Blair agreed that Homer had been a wanderer, adding that the strange experiences with which he had met had heightened the poet's enthusiasm and enabled him to write immortal epics.[2] Another critic, Lord Kames, said that the Homeric poems were too complex to have been created by a mere rhapsodist; he even thought it unlikely that they were ever sung or accompanied by the lyre. But, Kames adds, "Homer, in a lax sense, may be termed a bard," for he did travel about the country reciting, if not singing, his poems "to crowded audiences."[3] Whether or not this bard could write, Kames does not explicitly say. Like Beattie, he merely observes that "there is no appearance that writing was known in Greece so early as the time of Homer; for in none of his works is there any mention of it."[4]

Other critics did not apply the word "bard" to Homer but their emphasis upon inspiration and enthusiasm rather than orderliness of mind and calm judgment, upon qualities which they also found preëminent in Ossian, implies an unwillingness to think of him as a conscious artist. After enumerating some of the striking episodes in the *Iliad*, Ogilvie becomes rather indignant at the thought that many persons can give Homer "no higher praise than that of judgment" in the creation of these episodes.[5] He scorns the correctness which critics had so often found in Homer and applauds the Greek poet for having an "exuberance of an imagination inexhaustible in materials."[6] This criticism is not unlike that of Duff, who speaks again and again of the "variety," the "wildness," the "playful luxuriance of fancy,"[7] and the "astonishing display of imagination" in the *Iliad* and *Odyssey*.[8] In the latter poem he finds a kind of description which "wraps us in a pleasing and enchanting delirium."[9] But perhaps the most interesting estimate of the Greek poet was that made by Adam Ferguson. For him Homer is the "simple bard," without art or skill, moved by the "simple passions" of friendship, love, and resentment.[10] Vehement in his feelings, Homer speaks entirely from the heart "in

1. *Idem*, vi, 56; v, 91–2.   2. Blair, *op. cit.*, iii, 12–13.
3. Kames, *op. cit.*, i, 228.
4. *Idem*, i, 173. Beattie and Kames were apparently the only Scotch critics who even mentioned this important matter. D'Aubignac discusses it in his *Conjectures académiques* (1715); Rousseau, in his *Essai sur l'origine des langues*, and Robert Wood, in *An Essay on the Original Genius and Writings of Homer*, deal with the problem in some detail.
5. Ogilvie, *op. cit.*, i, 283–4, n.   6. *Idem*, i, 114, n.
7. Duff, *Critical Observations*, p. 184.   8. Duff, *Essay on Original Genius*, p. 24.
9. Duff, *Critical Observations*, p. 189.
10. Ferguson, *op. cit.*, pp. 265–6. Ferguson notes that "while we admire the judgement and invention of Virgil, and of other later poets, these terms appear misapplied to Homer."

words suggested by the heart: for he knows no other." Inspiration, not invention, a "supernatural instinct," not reflection—these guide him in his creation of poetry.[2]

This estimate of Homer is to be expected, of course. As I have suggested earlier, the Blackwellian supposition that Homer had described the manners of his age, that he had "painted what he saw," led critics to judge the poet by those manners. If Homeric society was considered barbaric and Homer had copied rather than created, it was to be assumed that the Greek poet was a kind of inspired bard or rhapsodist, having much in common with the bard who entertains Ulysses at the court of Alcinous and, in fact, with all men of his time. Emphasis upon sociological study and upon the environment and personal experiences of the poet (as suggested by internal evidence) had become so strong that the Scotch critics could not visualize the possibility that Homer had been a historian of a period more barbarous than his own, that several hundred years after the Trojan War, in a more advanced age, he had undertaken to describe a struggle between men whose characters seemed rather primitive to the poet himself. Even if the manners of Achilles and Hector were those of Homer's own time, these critics did not consider a second possibility: that the poet had been a shining light in a dark age, a calm and rational genius writing about violent kings and brutal warriors from experience, to be sure, but sharing in no way their primitive points of view. Finally, it did not occur to this group of writers that they might have interpreted Homeric society amiss, that other critics in past centuries had not been impressed by the barbarity of that society, nor had they seen any reason to characterize Homer as a rhapsodist.

Such an attitude toward Homer would probably have been much less common had it not been for the discovery of Ossian and a tendency to apply the same kind of criticism to both poets and to arrive at the same kind of result. Much more important is the fact that there were a number of writers who, in their eagerness to justify admiration for the Highland epics, intentionally drew all sorts of parallels between the two bards. A common way of making comparisons was merely to link their names together in some broad generalization. Thus John Macpherson says that "Ossian was the Homer of the ancient Highlanders,"[3] without offering any explanation of the statement. On another occasion he states that the Irish and Scotch have claimed that Ossian was a native of their countries in the same way that Asia and Europe contended "for the honour of having given birth

2. *Idem*, p. 266.
3. *Report of the Committee of the Highland Society of Scotland*, Henry Mackenzie, ed. (Edinburgh, 1805), Appendix, p. 15.

to Homer."[4] Before proceeding to an examination of *Fingal*, Ewen
Cameron says that Ossian was the "most celebrated Bard of *Caledonia*, as *Homer* was of *Greece*,"[5] and we find him again remarking
that Ossian "has been always reputed the *Homer* of the *Highlands*."[6]
Hume, who later believed that Ossian had never existed, observed
that the ancient Scotch poet sang the wars of Fingal just as the
Greeks sang the history of the struggle against Troy.[7] Again it was
possible for one to make an indirect comparison such as Brown made,
discussing Homer and Ossian in the same work and showing that each
lived and composed at the same stage in the development of poetry.
Still another way ·was to compare the qualities of mind and the
characteristics of the style of the two poets, often pointing out the
differences between them. Having described both as early bards,
Blair shows that Homer had greater ability in invention and in minute
descriptions, Ossian concentrating on "grand objects" and moving
rapidly from one object to another,[8] that Homer excels in "impetuosity and fire" and the narration of great battles, and Ossian in "the
pathetic" and in sentiment.[9]

But criticism of this kind was not fully convincing. To place Ossian
upon the pedestal which the Greek poet had occupied for "three
thousand years," mere descriptions of the relative merits of the two
bards were not sufficient; for it was too easy to disagree about "the
species of their sublimity," or "the beauties of expression," or the
kind of genius each possessed. The historical approach, on the other
hand, besides being more readily accepted by the Scotch critics of the
time, seemed to provide fewer points of controversy.

That this approach was considered more satisfactory than any
other is indicated by the fact that the use of other approaches was
extremely rare. Even when it was discovered that *Temora* had the
Aristotelian requisites for the epic, its formal elements were explained
historically. For example, James Macpherson observes that the poem
"resembles Homer" in the unities of time, place, and action, in the
narration of past events, in opening *in medias res*, and in the "working up" of the fable.[1] *Temora* may not have "all the *minutiae*, which
Aristotle, from Homer, lays down as necessary to the conduct of an
epic poem"[2] but all the "grand essentials" are present.[3] Now, since
Ossian was born in a remote country and time, it is obvious that he

4. John Macpherson, *Critical Dissertations on the Origin, Antiquities, Language,
. . . of the Ancient Caledonians* (London, 1768), p. 216.
5. Ewen Cameron, *The Fingal of Ossian* (Warrington, 1776), Preface, p. 21.
6. *Idem*, p. 8.
7. *The Letters of David Hume*, J. Y. T. Greig, ed. (Oxford, 1932), I, 329.
8. Hugh Blair, "A Critical Dissertation on the Poems of Ossian," in *Poems of Ossian*
(London, 1807), p. 171.
9. *Idem*, p. 118.   1. James Macpherson, *Temora* (London, 1763), p. 4, n.
2. *Ibid*.   3. *Idem*, p. 138, n.

knew nothing about Greek and Roman literature and had no more knowledge of the "rules" of composition than Homer had. In both cases, therefore, "the similarity must proceed from nature."[4] The two poets, besides living in the same stage in the progress of society, derived their ideas of the epic from the same source. But there are differences between them, Macpherson continues, almost all of which can likewise be explained historically. Since the one was a Greek and the other a Celt, "the compositions of Homer and Ossian are marked with the general and opposite characters of their respective nations."[5] Homer is lively and loquacious, while Ossian is concise in his expression.

Exactly the same kind of argument is advanced by Blair. Like Macpherson, he discovers that *Fingal* is an epic poem "even according to Aristotle's rules," since it has many of the formal elements of the *Iliad*.[6] This may seem astonishing at first. But one must remember that "Homer knew no more of the laws of criticism than Ossian,"[7] and that both, in writing after the same general plan, must have been guided by "nature." One must also remember that, in the beginnings of society, men are more alike than at any other time; and that, because Homer and Ossian beheld the same objects and passions, their poems must necessarily resemble one another. These realizations justify the critic in comparing the two poets and at the same time they offer reasons for the similarities between *Fingal* and the *Iliad*. On the other hand, if Homer is superior to Ossian in some respects— especially in avoiding monotonous repetitions—it should be understood that the Greek poet had viewed a larger number of "objects": prosperous cities, the beginnings of order and discipline, and the rise of the arts.[8]

Since it was assumed that Homer and Ossian had described only those things with which they had come in contact, it necessarily followed that they drew their characters in accordance with the nature of men in those times. In speaking of Ossian, Gregory says "*we must suppose, that the manners and sentiments he describes had their foundation in real life, as much as those described by Homer.*"[9] Not only was this true, Cameron remarks, but the manners and customs described by the poets are often similar, each portraying how the heroes killed and dressed their food, how they attended to domestic duties, how the young women of noble rank performed tasks which later ages ordinarily assigned to servants and slaves. "A thousand other Instances might be brought to shew the simple Manner in

---

4. *Idem*, p. 3, n.   5. *Idem*, p. 137, n.
6. Blair, "Critical Dissertation," in *Poems of Ossian*, p. 119.
7. *Idem*, p. 120.   8. *Idem*, p. 116.
9. John Gregory, *A Comparative View of the State and Faculties of Man with Those of the Animal World* (London, 1785), p. xi.

which People lived in early Times," he says by way of summary.[1] To Hume, Macpherson once said that the heroes of the "Highland epic" were like Homer's—"their own butchers, bakers, and cooks," as well as "their own shoemakers, carpenters, and smiths."[2]

No critic was more fully convinced than Duff that the two bards had copied the manners of men whom they had seen and heard. Since the Scotch heroes have the qualities of mind and body attributed to Homer's heroes, it is natural to assume that the circumstances of those ages were similar. Connal is "the Ulysses of Ossian," Duff observes,[3] and Fingal might well be compared to Hector. However, Ossian's knowledge was so restricted by the lack of travel and experience that he could have written twenty epic poems without being able to introduce characters substantially different from those of *Fingal*.[4] The kind of man he beheld, and hence the kind he wrote about, was for the most part engaged in similar occupations, in hunting and fishing. Though the period in which Homer composed his poems was "far from being polished," the "arts of civility" were at least more advanced and he was in a better position to portray all types of men. It would therefore be ridiculous to assume that Ossian could have described the variety of warriors and manners which we find in the *Iliad* unless he had actually "lived in the age and country of Homer."[5]

Whether or not Homer was thought to have had any advantages over Ossian depended primarily on whether or not the individual critic was a true primitivist. At least one writer, John Gordon, thought that the Greek bard was unfortunate in having lived so late in the development of Greek society. Can one believe that Homer copied from "nature," he asks, when one finds him using several dialects and characterizing heroes as gods and animals as monsters? Such deviations from "truth" indicate that he arrived upon the scene when manners and ideas were too refined to be used in epic poetry, "when men were too proud of art, to allow nature the first place."[6] But nothing of the sort was true in Ossian's case. In his poems one discovers a "great simplicity and attention to nature," proving that those poems were "written in a period of greater antiquity, than the *Iliad*" and that they were certainly composed "before art had reached that height, to which it had attained in *Homer's* time."[7]

If it was generally agreed that the Homeric poems belonged to a relatively refined age, one might expect that critics would find

1. Cameron, *op. cit.*, p. 22, n.   2. Greig, *op. cit.*, I, 330.
3. Duff, *Critical Observations*, p. 89.   4. *Idem*, p. 72.
5. *Idem*, p. 77.
6. John Gordon, *Occasional Thoughts on the Study and Character of Classical Authors* (London, 1762), p. 123.
7. *Idem*, pp. 109–12.

fewer signs of barbarism in those poems than in Ossian's. Actually, most critics discovered that there were more. Kames, for instance, says that in "Homer's time, heroes were greedy of plunder" and, "like robbers," insulted every enemy; while the Caledonians, on the other hand, were not addicted to thievery. When they conquered a foe, "their humanity overflow'd to the vanquished."[8] In courage, fidelity, independence, and largeness of soul, Gregory found the heroes of the two poets comparable; but Ossian's were undoubtedly superior *"in those gentler virtues of the heart, that accompanied and tempered their heroism."*[9] For Blair, the generous, humane "Fingal of the mildest look" had little in common with the mighty Hector. Tinctured "with a degree of the same savage ferocity, which prevails among all Homeric heroes," the latter rarely showed any compassion for a man whom he had conquered. Even when Patroclus was gasping for breath, Hector insulted his fallen enemy "with the most cruel taunts" and told him that in a short while his body would be devoured by vultures.[1] "War and bloodshed reign throughout the Iliad," Blair says, and the reader is provided little relief from the narration of battles and duels. While there is admittedly a great deal of fighting in Ossian, there are at least scenes showing the "tenderness of lovers" and "the attachment of friends, parents, and children"[2] to offset the martial ones. One reviewer of *Fingal* was surprised to find that the early heroes of Scotland were endowed with all the "delicacy of human nature," while the important characters of Homer were "mere barbarians, actuated by the most brutal revenge." Agamemnon is "imperious and insolent," he says, "Achilles fiery, puerile, vindictive, mercenary, and inhuman; Ulysses distinguished by low cunning."[3] There is scarcely one amiable hero in the entire Greek army, so far as this critic could see. Thinking of the same characters and the same descriptions which Blair had spoken of, Macpherson could scarcely refrain from calling Homer a barbarian. The human mind cannot dwell on the "protracted scene of carnage" in the *Iliad,* he says, without experiencing a feeling of disgust.[4] Nor can we compare the way in which the Greek and Scotch bards describe women without realizing that "Homer, of all ancient poets, uses the sex with least ceremony."[5] Certainly as far as the "dignity of sentiment" was concerned, all agreed that "the pre-eminence must clearly be given to Ossian."[6]

Also frequently compared were the systems of machinery used by Homer and Ossian. For example, Blair points out that the Greek poet "found the traditionary stories on which he built his Iliad, mingled

8. Kames, *op. cit.*, I, 438.　　9. Gregory, *op. cit.*, p. vii.
1. Blair, "Critical Dissertation," in *Poems of Ossian,* pp. 132–3.
2. *Idem,* p. 117.　　3. *Critical Review,* XII (December, 1761), 412.
4. Macpherson, *Temora,* p. 92, n.　　5. *Idem,* p. 206, n.
6. Blair, "Critical Dissertation," in *Poems of Ossian,* p. 119.

with popular legends concerning the intervention of the gods," and he adopted these legends because they amused the fancy of his audience. Similarly, Ossian "found the tales of his country full of ghosts and spirits"; he accepted the system because it was commonly accepted by the people of his time.[7] Since this latter species of the marvelous, did not interfere with human actions and since it was formed on a belief accepted in all countries in all ages, the Highland bard was perhaps more fortunate than Homer. He was at least not handicapped by a "light and gay mythology" and the traditionary accounts of squabbling gods and goddesses which the Greek poet was obliged to narrate.[8] Ossian's ghosts, Blair adds, are not unlike those we meet in the eleventh book of the *Odyssey*, and again in the twenty-third book of the *Iliad*, in which the spirit of Patroclus appears before Achilles. Precisely the same kind of comparison was made by Duff. While the invention and use of fabulous characters such as we find in the Homeric poems was "incompatible with the state of society in which Ossian lived," the Highland bard had his "ideal and supernatural beings" to employ as machinery.[9]

In the language and mode of expression of Homer and Ossian, parallels were again drawn. A modern language, Cameron says, is "unfit for poetical Composition"; it is too refined and employs too many "abstract Terms." But, in "the barren State of an uncultivated Tongue," the lack of such terms obliged the poet to use metaphors and similes, which animated poetry and helped to distinguish it from ordinary speech. Hence later ages have never succeeded in rivalling the language of the *Iliad* and *Odyssey*.[1] Hence, too, one may expect to find many similarities between Homer's manner of expression and that of Ossian. In abruptness, figurativeness, and vehemence, the writings of the Scotch poet bear "a remarkable Resemblance to the Poetry of the Eastern Countries," to the Old Testament and to "the Writings of *Homer*."[2]

Blair also compares the language and expression of the two bards but for the most part seems willing to dwell upon their differences. He observes, for example, that Ossian employs a greater variety of similes. While Homer confines the use of figures to martial subjects, the Highland poet also uses them to illustrate "the beauty of women" and "the different circumstances of old age, sorrow, and private dis-

7. *Idem*, p. 137.   8. *Idem*, p. 145.
9. Duff, *Critical Observations*, pp. 124–5.
1. Cameron, *op. cit.*, pp. 34–5. It was commonly thought that the similarities between Homeric and Ossianic language would be more apparent if the *Iliad* had been written in prose. Critics thought that Homer would have had fewer advantages over Ossian if this had been the case. It was perhaps no coincidence that Cameron published a verse translation of *Fingal* in 1771 and Macpherson a prose translation of the *Iliad* in 1773!
2. *Idem*, Preface, p. 23.

tress."[3] Macpherson finds a likeness between a particular speech of Malthos and the "laconic eloquence, and indirect manner of address" of Ajax in the ninth book of the *Iliad*. Finally, it was discovered that such epithets as "blue-eyed," "white-armed," "high-maned," "far-leaping," and "strong-hoofed" were present in the poems of each bard.[4]

From the arguments of these critics, one can see that a similarity between the formal elements of *Fingal* and the *Iliad* was in itself of minor significance and that, excepting Blair and Macpherson, most writers passed over such a similarity. What was really important to them was the fact that neither poet had derived his ideas from other poets, that he had written, on the other hand, as the circumstances of his time had obliged him to write—that he was an original genius. Because these geniuses imitated no one, because it was thought that similar societies produced similar poets, Homer was logically the poet with whom Ossian might best be compared. "Both wrote in an early Period of Society; both are Originals," Cameron said. As if these facts were to some degree responsible, he added: "both are distinguished by Simplicity, Sublimity, and Fire."[5]

It was, however, a strange situation in which these critics placed themselves. While they dogmatically proclaimed that the two bards copied the manners of an early stage of social development and that of the two Homer lived in a somewhat more refined period, they declared in the same breath that his characters were all savages compared to Ossian's! Actually, few writers seem to have realized what a dilemma these comparisons placed them in. They were either in too great an ecstasy over their new poet or they were too well occupied in defending him, along with the manners he portrayed, to see and to solve the difficulties involved in drawing parallels between the Greek and Highland epics. Amazed as they may have been that the manners of Ossian were so "civilized"[6] and that he expressed ideas suitable to the politest society, and skeptical as Hume may have been on those accounts,[7] it would appear that no one at this time thought of using the poems of Homer to argue against the authenticity of Ossian.

In some respects it was unfortunate for Homer that the name of Ossian was ever mentioned. Had it not been for this rival from the Highlands, the criticism of Blackwell and the Scotch studies of early poetry might have raised the reputation of Homer higher than it had

---

3. Blair, "Critical Dissertation," in *Poems of Ossian*, p. 198.
4. *Critical Review*, XII (December, 1761), 414.
5. Cameron, *op. cit.*, p. 25, n.   6. See Kames, *op. cit.*, I, 453.
7. Hume says that "the affected generosity and gallantry" of *Fingal* offers "striking proof" that the poems of Ossian were mere forgeries. (Green and Grose, *op. cit*, II, 417.) But it did not occur to him to use the Homeric poems to prove his point.

been for the past fifty years and more. He might have become the ideal primitive bard. Even so, whenever discussion concerned Homer alone, the Scotch did not censure him or his heroes or consider them particularly barbaric. Ferguson pointed out, for example, that, while the Greeks seem to have been "hunters of men," they were sufficiently civilized to understand the value of friendship. According to Beattie, Homeric language was not indicative of a time of barbarity, and even Kames, the severest Scotch critic of Homer, was pleased by the "lively pictures of ancient manners" and the Greeks' "natural way of life." In fact, for the very reason that it was not barbaric, the Homeric age had favored the creation of great epic poetry. Blair, we will recall, stated that whether or not one thoroughly approved of ancient manners they had afforded Homer the best possible materials with which to work, that (as Brown and Duff agreed also) human nature in Homer's time had been undisguised and natural, neither unpleasantly barbaric nor refined. Beattie was saying much the same thing when he remarked that the Trojan War and a state of society which was neither savage nor polite had inspired Homer to write immortal epics. Even the religion of the Greeks had aided Homer to a degree that Christianity could never have done. Finally, in speaking of Homer alone, the Scotch did not deny him inspiration, enthusiasm, imagination, or variety, qualities produced by a semibarbaric rather than a barbaric environment.

However, when the comparing of poets begins, this estimate of Homer is usually abandoned. What was said of Homer is now said of Ossian. Greek society is considered too advanced (Gordon) or too barbaric (Kames) to produce the best possible poetry. It can hardly win one's admiration in any case. Homer's heroes are called thieves, savages, lovers of revenge, and men without compassion, while Homer himself, as Macpherson says, delights in brutality and carnage. Even Greek mythology seems "light and gay" or ridiculous. Ossian, on the other hand, becomes the ideal primitive poet. He is mild and kind, one who respects women and parents. His heroes are humane and tender. His ghosts are also praised, if only because they do not, like Homer's, meddle in human affairs.

Other than the fact that both Homer and Ossian were epic poets of an early date, it would thus seem that sometimes the Scotch did not have many grounds for comparing the two. However, on rare occasions loyalty to Ossian did not call forth such sharp contrasts or, to put the matter more accurately, the desire to raise Ossian to Homer's level led the Scotch critics to speak of both differences and similarities without giving undue emphasis to either. It is at such times that their criticism shows some perspective and begins to foreshadow later critical theories. They then view Homer and Ossian as poets who live in societies which were about equally primitive, which were uncultivated enough to think more highly of bodily strength than of justice, and which fought wars for the same reasons. The heroes are even alike, for in the beginnings of society men seem to have the same passions and ideas. Duff remarks that Connal and Ulysses have much in common, and so do Fingal and Hector. While the Scotch realized, of course, that the Greeks were different from the Celts, they did not always find the one barbaric and the other refined. Nor was Homer always a barbarian compared to Ossian, for each was an ideal primitive poet, copying the manners and sentiments of real life in languages typical of societies at the same stage of development. Cameron remarked that "Ossian was the bard of Caledonia, as Homer was of Greece."

Behind all these interpretations of Homer and Ossian, and despite the inconsistencies, there is of course the Scotch view of history, a view which was partly old and partly new. Sometimes, particularly in speaking of Homer, the Scotch seem to regard the evolution of society in the way that earlier critics had, as a process covering the thousands of years since antiquity. One compares the high degree of refinement in modern times with the simplicity and naturalness of life in the Homeric or Ossianic periods. Another, in sympathy with the eighteenth century, contrasts Christianity and Christian morals with the paganism and immorality of Homer's age. However, it can be said, I think, that the writers who object to refinement are not usually so discontent with the present age as one is led to believe, hardly more so than those who glorify it. They were all able to see, as critics like Mme. Dacier apparently did not, that the age of Homer was not exactly a golden age, that it was warlike as well as peaceful. Nor did they think like Fénelon that it is almost impossible to reconcile some of the qualities of the Greeks with others. The Scotch, in fact, seeing the Homeric age as a whole, frequently approved of it only because it was favorable to the creation of great poetry, because bloodshed and strife had combined with peaceful, simple living to offer the poet a varied and highly interesting subject. Living in such an age was another matter.

It was new, this realization that a particular time in history was good for the poet but not necessarily for oneself. New also was the tendency of the Scotch critic, with a greater historical perspective than obtained among the French, to think of the development of individual societies as well as society in general. The Homeric age was not always considered as one extreme and the present age as another. According to the Scotch, the Greeks had risen by stages from barbarity to semibarbarity and then had reached a state of refinement in which all was art and sophistication. Except among the more fanatic worshippers of Ossian, it was generally agreed that Homer had lived in a semibarbarous time. As for Caledonian society, it too had gone through a similar development, and many other societies at different times and in different parts of the world had had the same kind of history. The Scotch then pointed out that poetry, or epic poetry at least, had attained perfection at one particular moment in this development—when, as Blackwell had said, art had tempered spontaneity and strife had given way somewhat to a semblance of order, when the best qualities of the "natural" man had become united with the best qualities of the civilized man. Homer and Ossian had both lived at this favorable moment in their respective societies and had therefore written poems of a similar kind. Comparison of the two is therefore possible, more possible, certainly, than comparison of either with poets of any society more advanced or less advanced.

While the Scotch were clearly as prejudiced as the Ancients and Moderns half a century earlier, trying equally hard to "prove" the superiority of a favorite poet, they had at least made considerable progress in developing the historical approach. They freed it, wisely or not, from other approaches with which it had been customarily combined and they pursued their historical interpretations about as far as one could without actually taking the point of view of the historical critic. Their influence on later literary criticism, and Homeric criticism in particular, was undoubtedly great, for their writings were popular, if not in England, at least in Germany. To later critics they suggested the possibility of using the new approach in a manner which could be either coldly historical and scholarly or, if one admired the early scenes of man and his naturalness, warmly romantic.[8]

8. Some comments by English critics have appeared in this chapter because they were so closely akin to comments made by the Scotch. Similarly, several Scotch and French writers are discussed in the next chapter, which deals primarily with English criticism of Homer.

V

English Historical Interpretations

AFTER the middle of the eighteenth century, it appears at first glance that the English critics as a group were less interested in Homer than were the critics of Scotland. The formalists and those who assumed a "rational" attitude toward poetry certainly had nothing vital to say about him. To discover their opinions of the Greek poet, in fact, one is usually obliged to search diligently through their works and to make a collection of vague, scattered remarks of an unoriginal nature.[1]

Homer was not forgotten, of course. But new critical standards had deprived antiquity of a monopoly upon poetic genius. A nationalistic spirit had encouraged appreciation of the early British poets and historical study had brought to the fore poets of whom previous generations had never heard. Homer was therefore faced with many new competitors. There were ever-increasing discoveries of new bards, new lyrists, or new writers of romances, some of whom merely drew attention away from Homer, while others were found to equal the Greek poet. Particularly after the appearance of Addison's later essays in the *Spectator,* an ever-growing number of English critics considered *Paradise Lost* superior to the Greek epics, and suggestions that Milton had borrowed many of his ideas and images from Homer or Virgil were welcomed with outbursts of indignation.[2] Likewise, following the publication of Lowth's *Praelectiones de sacra poesie Hebraeorum* (1753), more and more books of the Bible were accepted as poetry, and, significantly, poetry of a divinely inspired origin. Said one critic, Job "exceeds, beyond all comparison, the noblest parts of Homer," both in sublimity of thought and in schooling men in virtue.[3] As an unmoral or immoral poet, believing in the

1. Boswell maintains that Johnson was a great admirer of Homer. (*Boswell's Journal of a Tour to the Hebrides with Samuel Johnson,* Frederick A. Pottle and Charles H. Bennett, eds. [New York, 1936], p. 55, n.) Johnson's works are indeed full of allusions to the Greek poet, but those allusions are, for the most part, rather commonplace.

2. Lowth, for example, said that Milton was "the next in sublimity" after the Hebrew writers. Robert Lowth, *Lectures on the Sacred Poetry of the Hebrews,* G. Gregory, tr. (London, 1835), p. 279.

3. *Critical Review,* xxxv· (June, 1773), 450. The remark appeared in a review of Thomas Scott's *Book of Job in English Verse.* Speaking of Homer, another critic says, "when most on fire, how poor and inferior are his ideas of divine power, compared to those of the Scriptures." James Usher, *Clio; or, a Discourse on Taste Addressed to a Young Lady* (Dublin, 1778), p. 236.

mythology and inferior ethics of the pagans, Homer could hardly compete with the Hebrew writers, whose sublimity was owing to their knowledge of the true God and whose instruction was based upon a true understanding of right and wrong.

But neither Milton nor the Bible diverted as much attention from Homer as did the early English poets. "Shall we feel the fire of heroic poetry in translations from Greece and Rome, and never search for it in the native productions of our own country?" one critic asks with great eagerness.[4] The two or three mid-eighteenth-century editions of Spenser, Thomas Warton's *Observations on the Fairy Queen* and his *History of English Poetry*, Hurd's *Letters on Chivalry and Romance*, Percy's *Reliques*, and Mrs. Montagu's *Essay on the Writings and Genius of Shakespeare* are among the works which conclusively prove that new literary interests and standards, and perhaps the growth of English nationalism, were in part responsible for an indifference toward Homer. Because some critics who used the historical approach had shown that Aristotelian unity and design were not required in poetry in Spenser's day and because it was demonstrated that ghosts and witches were as acceptable when Shakespeare wrote as were nymphs and gods in ancient Greece, there was no longer any obvious reason to prefer the Greek poet to the early writers of England.

The same argument was used in justifying the practice of the Italian authors. Why should Tasso be censured for the figurativeness of his style, it was asked, if Homer could be forgiven for the "simplicity" of manners in the *Odyssey*? If Homer could use "the visible agency of the *Pagan* Deities," why ought Tasso, who also wrote in a superstitious age, to have avoided the use of "Magic and Enchantment" in his poems?[5] Questions of this kind were naturally welcomed by critics who were already convinced that the Italian's greatest merit lay in his fabulous episodes and "celestial visions"[6] and who believed with Voltaire that the *Gierusalemme liberata* was in every respect as admirable an epic as either of Homer's. The high praise of Tasso and Ariosto in the writings of major critics such as Hurd and Thomas Warton and lesser ones such as Mrs. Montagu and Pinkerton, as well as the translations of Tasso's poems by Hoole and Stockdale,[7] reveal

4. J. Aikin and A. L. Aikin, *Miscellaneous Pieces, in Prose* (London, 1773), p. 140.

5. John Hoole, *Jerusalem Delivered; an Epic Poem: Translated from the Italian of Torquato Tasso* (London, 1764), I, xvi. Hoole says, "If we do not, therefore, reject the poems of *Homer* and *Virgil* as not worth reading, because they contain extravagant fables, we have no right to make that a pretence for rejecting the JERUSALEM of *Tasso*." *Idem*, I, xvi–xvii.

6. *Hurd's Letters on Chivalry and Romance, with the Third Elizabethan Dialogue*, Edith J. Morley, ed. (London, 1911), p. 135.

7. Nor should one overlook the ephemeral enthusiasm for Richard Glover's *Leonidas* (1737) and William Wilkie's *Epigoniad* (1757).

the prevalent fondness for something very different from Homer.[8]

But, if the reputation of Homer suffered from sheer neglect and from invidious comparisons with English and Italian poets, it was also endangered by a revival of the time-worn arguments of the Moderns. The progressivists reiterated the contentions of Perrault and his allies that the earliest poet could hardly be the most perfect poet, that because Homeric manners were out-of-date they could be of little interest to the present age,[9] and that his machinery was ridiculous if not downright impious. As one facetious writer says, in speaking of the Greek deities, "we have the satisfaction to perceive, that their Godships are going out of fashion."[1] Not all critics may have agreed with John Gordon, who could recall scarcely one line in Homer which he had read "with sincere pleasure,"[2] but there were certainly a great many who were unable to find or to appreciate those universal elements of the *Iliad* for which earlier neoclassicists had prized the Greek poem so highly.

Fortunately for Homer, there were several reasons why he was not more completely ignored. It is clear that the historical approach was not the only approach which was being used. Nor should one forget that, however much the new demands for poetic originality discouraged the imitation of Homer, it was at the same time acknowledged that the Greek poet was one of the few original geniuses in the history of literature.[3] This realization at least appears to have raised him above Virgil, whose fire "is discovered as through a glass reflected from Homer."[4] Also, one must recognize the importance, however great or small, of Thomas Blackwell's book, the most systematic and complete attempt of the century to explain and justify the practice of Homer.

That the *Enquiry* was widely known in England as well as in Scot-

8. One critic remarks, "I see no reason why *the delivery of Persia by Cyrus* should not be a subject as interesting to us, as *the anger of Achilles*, or *the wandering of Ulysses*." William Jones, *Poems Consisting Chiefly of Translations from the Asiatick Languages* (Oxford, 1772), p. vii.

9. In a letter to Shenstone in 1759, Percy says that the "ancient Homerican Heroes are now worn so threadbare." *Thomas Percy und William Shenstone, ein Briefwechsel aus der Entstehungszeit der Reliques of Ancient English Poetry*, Hans Hecht, ed. (Strassburg, 1909), p. 22.

1. *Monthly Review*, XXII (February, 1760), 120.

2. (John Gordon), *A New Estimate of Manners and Principles: Being a Comparison between Ancient and Modern Times, in the Three Great Articles of Knowledge, Happiness, and Virtue; Both with Respect to Mankind at Large, and to This Kingdom in Particular* (Cambridge, 1760), p. 87, n.

3. Homer's reputation in the past also helped to maintain his popularity. Fairly common were such remarks as this: " '*Homer* is above detraction. . . . It is a sufficient test of his merit, that he has pleased every understanding age, in every country, for three thousand years.' " *Monthly Review*, IX (August, 1753), 102.

4. Ed. Watkinson, "An Enquiry into the Nature and Tendency of Criticism, with Regard to the Progress of Literature," *Critical Review*, XV (March, 1763), 163.

land may be gathered from the frequency with which it is mentioned by critics and scholars.[5] That it was also generally admired is indicated by the many references to Blackwell as an authority on ancient literature and by the many quotations from his book. Speaking of the professor of Greek, the Wartons, Hurd, Warburton, Mrs. Montagu, Gibbon, and others call him "an ingenious author" and "the learned and entertaining author of an *Enquiry into the Life and Writings of Homer*."[6] Now, the priority of Blackwell's work and the many citations from it do not prove that these authors were profoundly influenced by his criticism of Homer. But, considering the fact that the *Enquiry* appeared twenty years before the *Observations on the Fairy Queen*, there is some reason to believe that Warton and the others derived a few hints from Blackwell concerning the historical approach to literature. Remembering too that several of these men were critics of Homer and that their works on Shakespeare and Spenser in turn probably encouraged other persons to criticize the Greek poet from the same point of view, a certain importance must be conceded to Blackwell. It may at least be affirmed that he was the earliest of a large group of British critics to use the historical approach and that he was by no means unknown to those who came after him.

Among the most important indications of the influence of critics who made historical interpretations was the increasing desire for Homer in the original or at least in a literal translation, for Homer as he appeared to his contemporaries. It is significant, I think, that at least two earnest attempts were made to provide a better Greek text. Samuel Clarke's *Iliad* appeared between 1729 and 1732, and the *Odyssey* in 1740. Passing through numerous editions, his texts were for many years regarded as the best obtainable. But, as scholars continued to make emendations, a still more accurate text became desirable. Between 1756 and 1758, therefore, the Foulis brothers in Glasgow published a large, expensive edition of the Homeric poems, carefully edited and collated by the scholars Moor and Muirhead, a work which brought great applause from the magazines of the day. According to the *Monthly Review*, the Glasgow volumes constituted "as valuable an impression, as ever appeared in the Greek, or any other language,"[7] the writer adding that "admirers of Homer may read him in this edition with an increase of pleasure."[8] The *Critical Review*, in offering its praise, says that Homer's works should not "be rendered more forbidding to gentlemen, than must necessarily arise from the customs, manners and language of a people, that are

5. For a full treatment of the matter of Blackwell's popularity among the English critics, see Appendix.

6. It is rather interesting to note that almost all the critics who cited Blackwell constantly used a historical approach to literature.

7. *Monthly Review*, xx (March, 1759), 233.　　　8. *Idem*, xx, 234.

now no more."[9] Moor and Muirhead were to be thanked for removing many of the textual difficulties, the critic thought.

While some scholars were concerned with obtaining a correct Greek version, others were seeking to replace Pope's *Iliad* and *Odyssey* with English translations which would preserve the simplicity and enthusiasm of the Greek poet. Joseph Warton, for example, said that if an entire volume could be devoted to an examination of Pope's *Iliad,* one of its principal aims might be to show "how very inferior and unlike it is to the original, and how much overloaded with improper, unnecessary, and Ovidian ornaments."[1] Deploring the fact that some persons are so greatly pleased with this translation, Thomas Warton observes that readers have often been tempted "to acquiesce in the knowledge of Homer acquir'd by it, as sufficient."[2] Comments of this kind, of which there were a large number, stirred some of the would-be classicists to try new translations of the Homeric poems. One Samuel Ashwick[3] and one J. N. Scott[4] published single books of the *Iliad* in English in 1750 and 1755, respectively. Another attempt was made by a man named Samuel Langley in 1767.[5] Because all three were probably hoping for encouragement to translate the entire twenty-four books and because it was obvious that their versions were neither literal nor poetic, the magazines gave them long, unfavorable reviews, assuring them that Pope still reigned supreme. But almost every literary man rose in indignation when James Macpherson tried his hand in 1773. In his preface, the Scotchman labeled the earlier translations mere "paraphrases," inattentive to the "magnificent simplicity" of the Greek poet.[6] He considered his own "almost VERBATIM," a work designed to be "useful to such, as may wish to study the original, through an English medium."[7] Above all, he tried to preserve the spirit of Homer, not by writing as Homer would have written in the eighteenth century but by being as true to

9. *Critical Review,* III (June, 1757), 551.

1. Joseph Warton, *An Essay on the Genius and Writings of Pope* (London, 1782), II, 407, n.

2. Thomas Warton, *Observations on the Faerie Queene of Spenser* (London, 1754), p. 142. In the second edition, Warton says that "too many readers, happy to find the readiest accommodation for their indolence and their illiteracy, think themselves sufficient masters of Homer from Pope's translation." Thomas Warton, *Observations on the Fairy Queen of Spenser* (London, 1762), I, 198.

3. Samuel Ashwick, *The Eighth Book of the Iliad of Homer, Attempted by Way of Essay* (London, 1750).

4. Scott's work was entitled *An Essay towards a Translation of Homer's Work in Blank Verse, with Notes.* It was reviewed in the *Monthly Review,* XII (May, 1755), 355–70.

5. Samuel Langley, *The Iliad of Homer, Translated from the Greek into Blank Verse, with Notes Pointing out the Peculiar Beauties of the Original, and the Imitations of It by Succeeding Poets* (London, 1767).

6. James Macpherson, *The Iliad of Homer* (London, 1773), I, xxxi.

7. *Idem,* I, xxxv.

the sense of the original as possible. How badly he fared and how harshly he was criticized we need not stop to explain.[8]

Together with a broadening of literary interests and an increasing use of the historical approach, this desire to find out the true nature of the *Iliad* and *Odyssey*, to behold Homer as the ancients beheld him, to leave the atmosphere of the modern world for that of antiquity, led to the development of a more penetrating kind of criticism, a kind which went far beyond the superficial examinations and sweeping generalizations of Mme. Dacier. After all, it was realized, one can easily say that Homer copied the manners of his age, or that he accepted and used the religious system of the Greeks, or that it was "the fault of the age and not of Homer" if some of the poet's sentiments seem indelicate to us[9]—one can easily say these things without knowing much about the *Iliad* and *Odyssey* and certainly without contributing much to Homeric criticism. A deeper understanding of the poems, a willingness to view them from various angles, and a more rigorous application of the historical approach were therefore desirable.

Though none of these changes came about suddenly, one sign of this new development was the agreement among critics that it was by no means a simple matter to adopt the historical approach.[1] With more emphasis than any of the earlier writers, Voltaire says that modern customs and ways of thinking "sont plus différentes de celles des héros du siége de Troie que de celles des Américains. Nos combats, nos siéges, nos flottes, n'ont pas la moindre ressemblance; notre philosophie est en tout le contraire de la leur."[2] Owing to these momentous changes, modern readers inevitably struggle against "a secret Dislike" of the *Iliad:* they find themselves unable to penetrate the mists of antiquity successfully enough "to become the Contem-

---

8. For a review of Macpherson's translation, see *Critical Review*, xxxv (March, 1773), 161–76. Writing to William Mason on April 24, 1773, Richard Hurd says: "I have not looked into Macpherson's new translation. But I can conceive very well, how he might improve Ossian, & degrade Homer." *The Correspondence of Richard Hurd and William Mason, and Letters of Richard Hurd to Thomas Gray*, Earnest H. Pearce and Leonard Whibley, eds. (Cambridge, 1932), p. 87. A similar remark was made by Hume in writing to Adam Smith, April 10, 1773. He asks: "Have you seen Macpherson's Homer? It is hard to tell whether the Attempt or the Execution be worse." *The Letters of David Hume*, Greig, ed., II, 280.

9. Christopher Pitt and Joseph Warton, *The Works of Virgil, in Latin and English* (London, 1778), II, 11.

1. Also indicative of a new attitude was the popularity of works on antiquities. Often referred to in the eighteenth century were such works as Rollin's *De la Maniere d'enseigner et d'etudier les belles-lettres,* and John Potter's *Archaelogia Graeca.* First published around the beginning of the century, Potter's book reached a seventh edition by 1751.

2. "Essai sur la poésie épique," in *Oeuvres complètes de Voltaire* (Paris, 1877–85), VIII, 312–13.

poraries of *Homer*."[3] Most critics did not agree with Voltaire that it was impossible to understand the Greek poets; but they did issue warnings that one was likely to misinterpret them unless he properly employed the historical approach. Aware of the difficulties involved in attempting to criticize the ancients from the point of view of antiquity, Gibbon declares that the student of the early poets should possess "a circumstantial knowledge of their situation and manners."[4] Similarly, Joseph Warton states that it would be impossible to "relish" or adequately comprehend "any author, especially any Ancient," unless one constantly bore in mind the age, the country, and the climate in which the author lived;[5] and Spence observes that whatever seems to be a blunder "in such excellent writers as Homer and Virgil" should be attributed not to the poet's forgetfulness but to our ignorance "of some custom, or fact, very well known" in antiquity.[6]

Turning more directly to some of the estimates of Homer's poems, it might first of all be remarked that the same tendency persisted throughout the eighteenth century to idealize the manners and customs of the *Iliad* and *Odyssey* and to consider Homer a representative of the society which he describes. Joseph Warton, like Blackwell, was one of the greatest admirers of the Greek epics since the time of Mme. Dacier. He says of the *Odyssey* that its pictures of ancient laws, politics, customs, and domestic life render it "the most amusing and entertaining of all other poems"[7] and that the "primeval . . . simplicity of manners . . . is a perpetual source of true poetry,"[8] pleasing to all who are uncorrupted by the follies of life. The "simple supper" provided for Ulysses at the Phaeacian court, the gardens of Alcinous, Nausicaa performing the duties of a royal laundress are all objects worthy of the "dignity and simplicity of the Epic Muse."[9] Instead of describing "the most glittering lady in the drawing-room," as a modern poet would do, Homer portrayed the undisguised, unassuming princess as she danced among her maidens on the riverbank.[1] Warton becomes indignant because some critics have cen-

3. *Voltaire's Essay on Epic Poetry, a Study and an Edition*, F. D. White, ed. (Albany, N.Y., 1915), pp. 90–1.

4. Edward Gibbon, *An Essay on the Study of Literature* (London, 1764), p. 25.

5. J. Warton, *op. cit.*, I, 5.

6. Joseph Spence, *Polymetis: Or, an Enquiry Concerning the Agreement between the Works of the Roman Poets, and the Remains of the Antient Artists. Being an Attempt to Illustrate Them Mutually from One Another* (London, 1747), p. 56.

7. *The British Essayists*, Alexander Chalmers, ed. (London, 1802–03), XXIV, 246 (*Adventurer*, No. 80, August 11, 1753).

8. *Idem*, XXIV, 247. Warton declares that the *Odyssey* contains "the most lively and natural pictures of civil and domestic life, the truest representation of the manners and customs of antiquity," and that this poem is "the justest pattern of a legitimate Epopee." *Idem*, XXIV, 265 (*Adventurer*, No. 83, August 21, 1753).

9. *Idem*, XXIV, 246 (*Adventurer*, No. 80, August 11, 1753).   1. *Idem*, XXIV, 247.

sured the "natural strokes" which one finds scattered throughout the *Odyssey*. "They must needs nauseate the scenes that lie in Eumeus's cottage," he says, "and despise the coarse ideas of so ill-bred a princess as Nausicaa."[2]

Edward Gibbon also praised the simple manners of the heroic age and the "rusticity which gives so much delight, in Homer."[3] Even in reading the story of the fall of Troy, he says that we are pleased as by no modern author. In the single combats of chiefs, in the long discourses to the dying, one finds oneself becoming acquainted with the different heroes and becoming deeply concerned over their fate. Today, because of our vast armies, "machines animated by the breath of their General," it is impossible to create such amiable pictures of "the coward and the brave, the private centinel and the commander in chief."[4]

But the most celebrated admirer of ancient society, in either England or France, was of course Jean Jacques Rousseau. Émile and his mentor, having lost their way during one of their journeys, chance upon a country cottage occupied by an elderly man and his daughter. The master of the house receives them with such kindness that Émile cannot help exclaiming " 'quelle attention! quelle bonté! quelle prévoyance! et pour des inconnus! Je crois être au temps d'Homère.' " To this outburst his mentor replies that it is solitary existence which makes men welcome strangers and that in Homer's time " 'on ne voyageoit guère, et les voyageurs étoient bien reçus partout.' "[5] Later, when the four of them go out into the garden, Émile again finds a pleasant surprise awaiting him. " 'Le beau lieu!' s'écrie Émile plein de son Homère et toujours dans l'enthousiasme; 'je crois voir le jardin d'Alcinoüs.' " Sophie wonders who Alcinous was and is told that he was an ancient king who had a lovely daughter and that, the day after a stranger arrived at the palace, this daughter thought she would soon be married to him.[6] Poor Sophie blushes at this remark and blushes still more when her father—though he knew that she would have attended to all the laundering if it had been permitted —also explains that Nausicaa washed the clothes of the royal family in a river on the outskirts of the city.[7]

As in the time of Mme. Dacier, critics of the mid-eighteenth century made frequent comparisons between the customs and manners described by Homer and by the Hebrew writers of antiquity. For example, Thomas Scott observes that their descriptions of funeral rites had much in common, that if we examine the *Iliad* and *Job* to-

---

2. J. Warton, *op. cit.*, I, 401, n.   3. Gibbon, *op. cit.*, p. 33, n.
4. *Idem*, pp. 21–2.
5. "Émile, ou de l'éducation," in *Oeuvres complètes de J. J. Rousseau* (Paris, 1871–77), II, 385.
6. *Idem*, II, 391.   7. *Idem*, II, 392.

gether we shall find that it was customary in those times for the bereaved to sit upon the hearth and sprinkle his head with dust.[9]
When we read "qu'Abraham servit un veau à trois personnes" and
"qu'Eumée fit rôtir deux chevreaux pour le dîner d'Ulyssee," Rousseau
says,[10] we can easily see why the ancients were reputed great feeders.[1]
Husbands observes that the men of antiquity were usually given to
outward expression of sorrow, for Benjamin wept upon his brother's
shoulder even as the mighty Achilles sobbed in the presence of his
mother.[2] "The antient Manners are the natural Manners," one writer
declares;[3] and the clearest pictures of them may be found in the writings of the earliest of the Greeks and Hebrews.

Even more frequently likenesses were discovered between the
language and expression of Homer and the Bible.[4] With some hesi-
tation, Voltaire says "Si je l'osais, je comparerais l'Iliade au livre de
Job; tous deux sont orientaux, fort anciens, également pleins de fictions, d'images, et d'hyperboles."[5] Several times in the course of his
study of Biblical poetry, Lowth observes that the Hebrews derived
many of their metaphors from the occupations and experiences of
the shepherd and the farmer and that Homer, "who was uncommonly
fond of every picture of rural life," obtained many of his from the
same source.[6] For example, the Greek poet compares horses which
charge over the bodies of fallen warriors to steers which trample
down the grain. Though the Hebrews would probably have used the
simile in a different manner or for a different purpose, it is not unlike
the kind that they commonly employed and "approaches in some
degree the sublimity" of theirs.[7] In a discussion of Hebrew expressions, Hugh Blair says that "Homer is at least as frequent . . . in his
similes, founded on what we now call low life,"[8] and Hurd notes that
"numberless of the most beautiful *comparisons* in the Greek poet are
to be met with in the Hebrew prophets."[8a] While manifesting a
preference for the Biblical expressions, Thomas Scott says that "the
abrupt similes" which leave so much to the reader's imagination are

9. Thomas Scott, *The Book of Job, in English Verse; Translated from the Original Hebrew; with Remarks, Historical, Critical and Explanatory* (London, 1771), pp. 8, 15.
10. The Moderns had always expressed disgust at the quantities eaten by the early Greeks, even as they had disapproved of the fact that Homer's heroes cooked their own food.
1. "Essai sur l'origine des langues," in *Oeuvres de J. J. Rousseau*, I, 386.
2. J. Husbands, *A Miscellany of Poems by Several Hands* (Oxford, 1731), Preface.
3. François Ignace Espiard de Laborde, *The Spirit of Nations, Translated from the French* (London, 1753), p. 351.
4. Earlier critics had merely implied that these likenesses existed.
5. "Dictionnaire philosophique," in *Oeuvres complètes de Voltaire*, xx, 411.
6. Lowth, *op. cit.*, p. 73.   7. *Ibid.*
8. "The Poetry of the Hebrews," in *Lectures on Rhetoric and Belles-Lettres*, p. 465.
8a. "On Poetical Imitation," in *Q. Horatii Flacci Epistolae ad Pisones, et Augustum: with an English Commentary and Notes: to Which Are Added Critical Dissertations* (Dublin, 1768), II, 144.

found in all Eastern writings,[1] particularly in the *Iliad* and in the *Old Testament*.[2]

Because all this criticism of Homeric times and the comparisons of Homer and the Bible added little to what Fénelon and Mme. Dacier had already said, it is not to the purpose to elaborate upon these matters. It will be sufficient to keep in mind the fact that most of those who considered Homer a representative of a golden era and who compared Homeric and Biblical simplicity of manners and of language perpetuated the ideas of earlier critics. But there were new and important conceptions of the *Iliad* and *Odyssey*, many of which undoubtedly grew out of these romantic views of ancient poetry. What, it was asked, is the essential difference between the *Odyssey* and the medieval romance? With his gift of a boundless imagination, was it correct to say that Homer was a conscious composer of epics? Was the use of a particular *form* the only thing which separated him from other tellers of tales?

As early as 1712 Addison had observed that reading the *Iliad* is like travelling through an uninhabited land, in which one's fancy "is entertained with a thousand Savage Prospects of vast Desarts, wide uncultivated Marshes, huge Forests, mishapen Rocks and Precipices."[3] To most of us this might just as easily be a description of the *Faerie Queene;* and, in fact, Addison does make an indirect comparison of the poems of Homer and Spenser in another essay. Referring to the travel stories of John Mandeville and Ferdinand Mendez Pinto, he says that one peruses them "with as much astonishment as the travels of Ulysses in Homer, or of the Red-Cross Knight in Spenser. All is enchanted ground and fairy-land."[4] A few years later, John Hughes remarked that in describing Achilles' speaking horse and Xanthus, the speaking river, Homer had merely intended "to fill the Reader with Astonishment and Concern." The same was probably true of the stories of Scylla, Charybdis, and the sirens, though, as in Spenser, there were obviously allegorical meanings attached to these particular episodes.[5]

At a time when Terrasson, Hardouin, and Blackwell were trying to interpret the allegory of Homer, it is not surprising that some critics

1. Another writer finds the same "strains of sublimity" in Homer and the Bible. John Newberry, *Art of Poetry on a New Plan: Illustrated with a Great Variety of Examples from the Best English Poets; and of Translations from the Ancients* (London, 1762), I, 21. J. Warton compares Homeric and Biblical description. *Works of Virgil,* II, 329, n. See also Husbands, *op. cit.,* Preface.

2. T. Scott, *op. cit.,* p. 137, n.

3. *The Spectator,* Smith, ed., Vol. III, No. 417, p. 79.

4. *The Tatler,* George A. Aitken, ed. (London, 1899), Vol. IV, No. 254, p. 288.

5. John Hughes, *The Works of Mr. Edmund Spenser. In Six Volumes, with a Glossary Explaining the Old and Obscure Words* (London, 1715), I, xl. Hughes observes that the "Mutability cantos" have "several Strains of Invention" which are "not unworthy of *Homer* himself." *Idem,* I, xci.

were pointing out the similarities between the Greek and English poets. If Vulcan represented the armorers, and Circe was intemperance, and Aphrodite was a personification of human lust, the *Iliad* and *Odyssey* had at least something in common with the *Faerie Queene*.[6] However, most writers followed Addison, and comparisons with respect to allegory were not made nearly so often as comparisons with respect to the marvelous.

Even the neoclassicists had admitted that Homer's poems contained many amazing fictions. To these they attributed much of the poet's sublimity and variety, and it was only on rare occasions that anyone raised objections to a discreet use of fabulous episodes. Drawing a sharp distinction between the probable fictions of Homer and the improbable ones of the Italian poets, they had proclaimed that the one type was to be admitted in the epic and the other to be rejected. But the eighteenth century soon began to have doubts about the Homeric episode. What, it was asked, was so probable about the story of men turned into swine? What, on the other hand, was so improbable about the tales of the Italian poets and why were they more improbable than Homer's? Finally, how could there be any hard and fast rules concerning the use of fables, for fables were merely intended to please the imagination of the reader?[7]

To mention a few of the comments of the mid-eighteenth-century critics, Voltaire said that Ariosto and Homer had "l'intempérance de l'imagination, et le romanesque incroyable";[8] and Blair declared that Tasso was "not more marvellous and romantic" than Homer, the difference between them being that "in the one we find the romance of paganism, in the other, that of chivalry."[9] Even Warburton contributed a comment of this kind. He said that Homer had written "a *military* and *civil* Romance, brimfull of fabulous trumpery."[1] Because of his "violent machinery" and the "extravagant sallies of his imagination,"[2] Clara Reeve called Homer "the parent of Romance."[3]

6. In speaking of the allegorical nature of the *Faerie Queene*, Newberry says that "the *Iliad* and *Odyssey* of Homer are said to be fables of this kind," the gods and heroes being the visible shapes of "the affections of the mind." Newberry, *op. cit.*, II, 32.

7. One critic pointed out that in many respects "the *Old Romance* may be considered as a kind of Epic." For example, in both "truth is apparently violated," and violated intentionally. Chalmers, *op. cit.*, XXIII, 19 (*Adventurer*, No. 4, November 18, 1752).

8. "Essai sur les moeurs et l'esprit des nations et sur les principaux faits de l'histoire depuis Charlemagne jusqu'a Louis XIII," in *Oeuvres complètes de Voltaire*, XII, 247.

9. Blair, *Lectures on Rhetoric and Belles-Lettres*, p. 497. According to Hurd, both Homer and Pindar were "ancient masters of romance." Morley, *op. cit.*, pp. 55–6.

1. William Warburton, *The Divine Legation of Moses Demonstrated* (London, 1765–66), IV, 352, n. He also speaks of "*Homer's* military and Political Romances."

2. Clara Reeve, *The Progress of Romance, through Times, Countries, and Manners; with Remarks on the Good and Bad Effects of It, on Them Respectively; in a Course of Evening Conversations* (London, 1785), I, 20.

3. *Idem*, I, 19.

Why should the romances be scorned, she asks, when the fables of the classical authors are much wilder than any others?[4] According to Hurd, Homer's Circe and Calypso were overcome by the Greek hero even as the medieval knight overcame the charms and enchantments of mysterious women;[5] and, in the same vein, Joseph Warton pointed out that the writers of romances depended upon the poets of antiquity, that their monsters, magicians, and invulnerable warriors were copied from the Circe, Medea, Achilles, and the sirens of ancient Greece. "The cave of Polypheme," he says, "might furnish out the ideas of their giants."[6]

If it was believed that later poets had merely imitated the marvelous episodes of Homer, the comparisons of the *Odyssey* and the romance would be of less importance to us. But we find that the similitudes were sometimes given historical explanations, explanations based upon the particular circumstances obtaining in ancient Greece and medieval Europe. Fabulous stories, the critics said, are the delight of all rude ages. Before reason has destroyed the mystery of the world, before experience proves that nature does not produce such terrifying beings as dragons and ghosts and one-eyed giants, men permit their fancies to roam, to invent strange tales, and to attribute superhuman qualities to the heroes of those tales. The romance and the heroic fable, said Clara Reeve, were the "favorite entertainment" of early societies.[7] At first the tales were based upon actual events and concerned actual men, and were listened to with the undivided attention of every audience. In time, however, the noble deeds of mortals were elaborated upon and were ascribed to the gods; and allegory concealed the historical facts. Since the stories were still highly "agreeable fictions,"[8] poets continued to use them until Homer finally gave them "a regular model or form."[9] Having "the same root" and describing the same actions for the same purpose, the romance and the epic are not essentially different.[1]

Hurd also had something to say about the origin of the marvelous. "When the received system of manners or religion in any country, happens to be so constituted as to suit itself in some degree to this extravagant turn of the human mind," then poetry will elaborate upon

4. *Idem*, I, 21. Duff did not call Homer a writer of romances but he frequently emphasized the marvelous nature of his episodes. He says they are "highly pleasing" and "most surprising fictions." Duff, *Critical Observations on the Writings of the Most Celebrated Original Geniuses in Poetry*, pp. 8–9. Speaking of the grotto of Calypso, he says that "we are transported into this ideal region" and wander through it "absorbed in wonder and delight." *Idem*, p. 62.

   5. Morley, *op. cit.*, pp. 99–100.   6. J. Warton, *Essay on Pope*, II, 3.

   7. Reeve, *op. cit.*, I, 13–14.   8. *Idem*, I, 15.   9. *Idem*, I, 29.

   1. *Idem*, I, 16. Speaking of the strange adventures of heroes, Reeve says that "In the history of *Sindbad*, we have most of those that *Ulysses* meets with in the Odyssey: insomuch that you must be convinced the likeness could not be accidental." *Idem*, I, 22–3.

those wonders and will possess the distinctive qualities of the pagan fable and the Gothic romance.[2] Similarly, Beattie applied to the romance the same observation which Blackwell had made about the origin of the Homeric episodes. Being unable to ascertain exactly what had occurred in other ages and in distant lands, men gave credit to anything that was reported to them.[3] They believed that monsters and witches really did exist, for the simple reason that some people said they had seen them. Hence the poet, intent upon pleasing his listeners, was obliged to describe such creatures in his narrations.[4]

The critic who most earnestly endeavored to explain the similarities between Homer's poems and the romance was, of course, Richard Hurd. Instead of dwelling upon the love for the fabulous in ancient Greece and medieval Europe, Hurd sought an explanation in the realm of political and social circumstances. He says that " 'there is a remarkable correspondency between the manners of the old heroic times, as painted by their great romancer, Homer, and those which are represented to us in the books of modern knight-errantry.' "[5] For Greece, like France and England in the Middle Ages, was divided into a number of independent feudal governments among which there was continual warfare. Because of the strife and petty jealousies and acts of vengeance which he beheld on all sides, it was only natural that the poet, whether a writer of epics or of romances, should constantly describe "battles, wounds," and "deaths,"[6] that his compositions should be full of all kinds of images derived from the experiences of the warrior. Homer's Laestrygonians and Cyclops, Hurd said, were nothing more than "bands of lawless savages," and the Greek heroes of antiquity were "the exact counter-parts" of Lancelot and Amadis of Gaul.[7] In both eras there were "private adventurers" who redressed the wrongs committed against the weaker kings, who made it their task to seize the possessions of an aggressor.[8] In both eras there was the same desperate need for the union of warring states against a common foe. Finding dissensions among the chiefs of the various Greek communities and desiring to bring about unanimity, Homer exposed in the *Iliad* "the capital mischiefs and inconveniences" arising from their disagreement; and in the *Odyssey* he revealed the insolent behavior of the subjects of these chiefs when the latter were absent on military expeditions. We find that similar

2. "On the Idea of Universal Poetry," in *Q. Horatii Flacci Epistolae*, II, 6.
3. "On Fable and Romance," in *The Works of James Beattie*, III, 24–5.
4. Thomas Warton observes that "TALES are the learning of a rude age." Before manners are refined and men attain any considerable degree of speculative knowledge, stories are used instead of subtle arguments to convey knowledge to the populace. Thomas Warton, *The History of English Poetry, from the Close of the Eleventh Century to the Commencement of the Eighteenth Century* (London, 1840), I, cxxxix.
5. Morley, *op. cit.*, pp. 94–5.   6. *Idem*, p. 95.
7. *Idem*, p. 98.   8. *Idem*, p. 100.

conditions prevailed in medieval times, that during the Crusades "the designs of the confederate Christian states were perpetually frustrated, or interrupted at least, by the dissensions of their leaders,"[9] and that meaner men at home often attempted to usurp the authority of their superiors.

Now, the idealization of ancient society and the comparisons between Homer and the Bible, and particularly between Homer and the romance, might have contributed something to a new attitude toward the Greek poet and might at least have aided in discouraging the neoclassical conception of the *Iliad* and *Odyssey*. Though it was clear that the Homeric poems were more carefully planned than the average romance, that the parts of each more evidently belonged to a single great action, there can be little doubt that the accentuation of the purely narrative and marvelous elements of the poems and the conviction that Homer was a teller of exciting and romantic tales did not encourage the belief that the Greek poet was a conscious artist. Yet one cannot grant that criticism of this kind was responsible for the attitude toward Homer and his poems which developed later in the century. Much more important, I think, were the views of the English and French critics of the ballad, the views of the political and social historians, and the views of persons who had no illusions about the glorious simplicity of Homeric times. Through their criticism and through the criticism of the Scotch writers arose the conception of Homer as a primitive singer.

In the opinion of many, the age of Homer was not the golden era of the world, a period when happy princes tended their flocks and rejoiced in the savory odors of flesh broiling on the campfire, and maidens shrieked with delight as they played ball in the meadows beside the river. It was not even a primitive age, an age of "noble savages," of war and heroism, of feuds and noble deaths, of blood and glory. For these critics thought that Homer's compatriots had all the bad qualities of the American Indians, the Peruvians, or the African tribesmen, with few of the good qualities which the eighteenth century often attributed to those people. One critic, for instance, speaks of Achilles as "a boisterous, rapacious, mercenary, cruel, and unrelenting brute"[1]—harsh words for the hero whom the neoclassicists admired as the epitome of hospitality, courage, and friendship! Commenting on the description of battles in the *Iliad*, another critic, a physician, remarks that "a slaughter-house or a surgery would not seem proper studies for a poet."[2] Homer and "his imitators," he says,

9. *Idem*, p. 106.
1. John Jortin, "On the State of the Dead, as Described by Homer and Virgil," in *Six Dissertations upon Different Subjects* (London, 1755), p. 214.
2. Aikin and Aikin, *op. cit.*, p. 167. Our critic says that the early poets "considered the human body with anatomical nicety."

"dwelt with a savage pleasure upon every idea of pain and horror that studied butchery could excite."[3] When the Greek poet describes Achilles sacrificing Trojans to the manes of Patroclus, Voltaire declares, "C'est à peu près l'histoire des premiers barbares que nous avons trouvés dans l'Amérique septentrionale."[4] The ancient inhabitants of Greece were mere "sauvages superstitieux et sanguinaires," he adds;[5] and their poets were bards who sang about the deeds of "guerriers très-grossiers vivant de rapine."[6]

When he made this criticism, Voltaire possibly had in mind a book on the American savage published a few years before his own *Essai*, Lafitau's *Moeurs des sauvages*. This work became well known later in the century and was often cited by the Scotch primitivists.[7] Following a discussion about the manners and customs of the Indians, Lafitau makes such interesting remarks as this: "Homere, Dyctis de Crête, & Darés Phrygien, nous fournissent plusieurs exemples de la brutale ferocité de leurs Héros, qui portant leur haine audelà des termes de la vie, s'acharnoient sur les corps de leurs ennemis morts, & leur faisoient toutes sortes d'insultes."[8] Speaking of the cruel way in which Achilles drags Hector's body around the Trojan walls and of the unbelievable savagery of warriors on both sides, he asks, "Quoi de plus inhumain que les Héros de l'Iliade?"[9] Lafitau implies that they were at least no more civilized than the redskins.

A similar attitude was taken by two contributors to the magazines. In reviewing a recent piece of Homeric criticism, Goldsmith finds occasion to discuss the "barbarous" manners of the *Iliad*, most of which, he says, are entirely displeasing to the modern reader and are productive of feelings of "horror and disgust."[1] However, it was not Homer's fault if he fails to satisfy the present age, for he wrote when "barbarity, ignorance, lust, and cruelty, were still in fashion,"[2] when "all those instances of cruelty" were in no way offensive to men.[10]

3. *Idem*, pp. 166–7.
4. "Les Loix de Minos," in *Oeuvres complètes de Voltaire*, VII, 177, n.
5. Goguet notes that, "comme les Sauvages," the Greeks "mangeoient prodigieusement." Antoine Yves Goguet, *De l'Origine des loix, des arts, et des sciences; et de leurs progrès chez les anciens peuples* (Paris, 1758), II, 382.
6. Voltaire, *loc. cit.*
7. Brown constantly cites Lafitau in his *Dissertation on Poetry and Music*, and Millar quotes him several times in his *Origin of the Distinction of Ranks*.
8. Lafitau, *Moeurs des sauvages ameriquains, comparées aux moeurs des premiers temps* (Paris, 1724), II, 427–8.
9. *Idem*, II, 287.
1. *Critical Review*, IX (January, 1760), 17. Goldsmith was reviewing R. Kedington's *Critical Dissertations upon the Iliad of Homer*. For a discussion of the grounds upon which the article is attributed to Goldsmith, see R. S. Crane's "A Neglected Mid-eighteenth-Century Plea for Originality and Its Author," *Philological Quarterly*, XIII (January, 1934), 21–9.
2. *Critical Review*, IX, 13. Goldsmith says, "These barbarous manners tincture his whole poem." *Ibid.*   10. *Idem*, IX, 17.

Once in the course of his essay, Goldsmith indirectly compares Homeric society with that of the savages. Speaking of the not-too-pleasant episode in which the infant Achilles is said to have vomited wine upon the clothes of Phoenix, he says that travellers who are acquainted with "barbarous nations at this day, find delicacy of idea or language scarcely known among them" and find that savages never attempt to express themselves by means of "circumlocutions."[4]

A similar estimate of ancient society and poetry is made by a writer in the *Monthly Review*. He too dwells upon the "ignorance and barbarity" of Homeric times,[5] concluding with the statement that, like Homer's heroes, "the savage Indians insult their vanquished enemies," and "sing and dance round them, and mortify them with every kind of brutal raillery."[6] Objectionable as the description might be, this critic agreed with Goldsmith (and Bayle) that the episode concerning Achilles' loss of the wine would not appear disgusting to "a rude and unpolished people."[7]

There were other ways of showing that Homer was a representative of a savage nation. Because Helen was valued no more than the treasure which had been stolen with her and because she was little more than one of Menelaus' personal possessions, Millar says that the Greeks had certainly not attained "any high degree of delicacy," that there is every reason for believing they had not "entirely shaken off their ancient barbarous manners."[8] The practice of stripping the dead, the ferocity of the Greek soldier in time of war, and the cruelty of the hero even in time of peace were accepted as indications of the savagery of the Homeric age.[9] According to Goguet, one is seized with horror in perceiving "l'esprit de barbarie & de cruauté" which reigned in those days,[1] in seeing how men massacred, enslaved, plundered, and burned. But if we lack sufficient evidence that the age of Homer was ignorant and barbaric, the credulity of the people and their belief in oracles can be pointed to as absolute proof. For the kind of superstition which prevailed among the Greeks is always to be associated with primitive peoples: "témoins les Sauvages, qui n'entreprennent rien que préalablement ils n'aient consulté leurs divins &

4. *Idem*, IX, 16. Goldsmith says "heroism was never worse known than in those ages which were called heroic." *Idem*, IX, 13. Bayle probably inspired some of these comments. He criticized harshly the Phoenix-Achilles episode.

5. *Monthly Review*, XXII (February, 1760), 120–1. The reviewer is thought to be Owen Ruffhead.

6. *Idem*, XXII, 126.   7. *Idem*, XXII, 124.

8. John Millar, *The Origin of the Distinction of Ranks; or an Inquiry into the Circumstances Which Give Rise to Influence and Authority in the Different Members of Society* (Basil, 1793), p. 66. The book was first published in 1771.

9. See Claude François Xavier Millot, *Elements of General History. Translated from the French* (Worcester, Mass., 1789,) I, 142. One of Millot's chapters is entitled "Barbarism of the Heroick Ages; Superstitions, &c."

1. Goguet, *op. cit.*, II, 370.

leurs oracles."[2] Having considered some of these facts, Goguet decides that it would be needless to prove that "les éloges dont certains Auteurs ont jugé à propos de combler les tems héroîques, sont faux & déraissonables."[3]

From the arguments of this group of critics and from the remarks of Joseph Warton and Rousseau, we can see that opposing views could be taken of Homer's poems and we can also see how the estimate of the poet himself might to some extent depend upon one's interpretation of his poems. Rousseau, thinking mainly in terms of the *Odyssey*, was an enthusiastic admirer of Homer; Goldsmith, considering the struggle around Troy (and perhaps some of the Indian wars), had little sympathy for so barbaric a poet.

But, leaving aside all matters of likes and dislikes, idealizations and condemnations, other significant developments of the mid-eighteenth-century criticism of Homer must now be examined—developments which were to have a far-reaching effect. As previously suggested, there was an increasing tendency among a certain group of writers to ignore the *Iliad* and *Odyssey* as literature, to look beyond them to the society which they represented. Viewing the two poems as social documents of a distant age, these critics were primarily interested in the way of life, in the significance of certain manners and customs and modes of thought, of the ancient Greeks. Indeed, such pursuits may seem to belong to the antiquarian and the pedant. But this group did not usually confine itself to discussions of unimportant points, to quibbling about the allegory behind the Greek representations of Zeus or Vulcan, or to arguing about the precise value of a dozen cattle in Homeric times; for these men belonged to that widespread movement of the eighteenth century which had for its aim a closer understanding of the early societies of the world. At a time when Gibbon was occupied with his *Decline and Fall of the Roman Empire,* when Robertson was writing the histories of Scotland and America, and when Voltaire was treating the period of Charles XII, it was natural that some persons should manifest an interest in the early ages of Greece. Since the cultural characteristics of a society were considered as important as its political history and since there were few original sources for a study of the ancient Greeks, it was also natural that writers should turn to the *Iliad* and *Odyssey* of Homer.

Now, the fact that men of letters were sometimes as interested in what the poems represented as in the proper appreciation of the poems themselves proves that the scholar and the historian were not

2. *Idem*, ii, 55.
3. *Idem*, ii, 393. The Greeks were slow in making any advances, Goguet says, but the fact that a Homer arose soon after the Trojan War shows that they did not neglect the arts entirely. *Idem*, ii, 289–90.

alone responsible for this type of approach. Instead of solely emphasizing the sublimity of the noble sentiments of the poet, Thomas Warton values early literature in part because it gives the modern reader an opportunity to trace man's "transitions from barbarism to civility";[4] and another critic says that it "is pleasing to mark the first dawnings of science, and to trace the gradual advancements of it . . . to view the least propensity to rational pursuits, amidst a cloud of impenetrable ignorance and superstitious absurdity."[5] Though Homer wins our esteem because he is one of the world's greatest poets, the fact that he is the most ancient author of the pagans entitles him to "a primary regard in the annals of literature."[6] For Johnson the famous shield of Achilles was important primarily because it "shows a nation in war, a nation in peace; harvest sport, nay, stealing."[7] A similar attitude was taken by Monboddo in a discussion about Homeric characters with Johnson, the former observing that the "'history of manners is most valuable.'"[8] As it was pointed out earlier, Joseph Warton valued the *Odyssey* for its pictures of primeval domestic life, of the way men lived in the first ages of the world; and in his *Essay on Pope* he agrees with Monboddo that "the most important part of all history" is "the *History of Manners*."[9] Likewise Hurd observes that "the almost infinite variety of images and pictures" in the Homeric epics has been extolled by many critics. In the *Iliad* and *Odyssey*, he says, are poetic figures and descriptions derived from every art which men had "invented for the service or ornament of society."[1] Even Clara Reeve, though no student of the classics, attributed part of her pleasure in reading Pope's translation of Homer to its representation of the "History and Manners of the times" in which the poet lived.[2] Finally, Mrs. Montagu notes that Homer "has enriched" his epics with mythology, the fine arts, "and whatever adorned the mind of man, or blest society" in that early age.[3]

While the literary critics were showing their enthusiasm for the *Iliad* and *Odyssey* as pictures of antiquity, the scholars and historians were making use of the poems to draw more specific conclusions about the mode of life in the heroic ages. Guys, for example, says that Homer "sera toujours la plus pure source de toute l'Antiquité

4. T. Warton, *History of English Poetry*, I, 3, Preface.
5. Watkinson, *op. cit.*, xv, 162–3.   6. *Idem*, xv, 163.
7. Pottle and Bennett, *op. cit.*, p. 54.   8. *Idem*, p. 55.
9. J. Warton, *Essay on Pope*, II, 208. Lafitau had said, "La science des Moeurs & des Coûtumes des differens Peuples a quelque chose de si utile & de si interessant, qu'Homere a cru devoir en faire le sujet d'un Poëme entier." Lafitau, *op. cit.*, I, 4.
1. "On Poetical Imitation," in *Q. Horatii Flacci Epistolae*, II, 124–5.
2. Reeve, *op. cit.*, I, 19–20.
3. Elizabeth Montagu, *An Essay on the Writings and Genius of Shakespear, Compared with the Greek and French Dramatic Poets, with Some Remarks upon the Misrepresentations of Mons. de Voltaire* (Dublin, 1778), p. 23.

Grecque" for a study of primeval customs and manners,[4] and Millot speaks of Homer as "the great painter of ancient manners."[5] Besides considering the Greek poet an "observateur exact du Costume" of early society, Goguet draws almost all of his information about the life of the ancients from the Homeric poems; and Adam Smith used the two epics in his lectures to illustrate one particular stage in the social development of man. For instance, he says that jealousy was virtually unknown in the "rude and uncultivated" country of Homer because there was no sentimental relationship between the sexes and that it was merely because Helen had been carried away by force that Menelaus became indignant and plunged all Greece into a long struggle.[6] But war was the delight of the early Greek communities, Millar pointed out. They were constantly at odds, often over nothing more consequential than the theft or seduction of a wife or daughter.[7] Barbarous though Homer's predecessors might be, Millar observed that they made some progress in the military art, since they had found it more successful to use the "cunning of a Ulysses" to deceive an enemy than to employ "the brutal force of an Ajax" to overpower him with sword and spear.[8] Some writers, including Goguet, Kames, Guys, Lafitau, and Mitford, made exhaustive examinations of the *Iliad* and *Odyssey* to determine what domestic arts were known to Homer, what kinds of scientific discoveries had been made, and what kinds of architecture had been developed among the ancient Greeks.

While Homer was considered the historian of manners, he was also considered the political historian of an early society—in fact, the only one of that period whose works are extant. This was no new and startling discovery, of course. But, at a time when people were becoming more and more deeply interested in the past, it was perhaps natural that writers should give the point greater emphasis than ever. Before the invention of writing, Turgot explained, songs were the only means of preserving the memory of important events; and these songs, even after it was possible to record them, continued to retain their half-historical, half-fabulous character. Homer knew that "les

4. P.-A. Guys, *Voyage littéraire de la Grèce, ou lettres sur les Grecs, anciens et modernes, avec un parallèle de leurs moeurs* (Paris, 1783), I, 381. The book was translated into English under the title *A Sentimental Journey through Greece* and an edition was published in Dublin in 1773.

5. Millot, *op. cit.*, I, 141.

6. *Lectures on Justice, Police, Revenue and Arms, Delivered in the University of Glasgow by Adam Smith, Reported by a Student in 1763*, Edwin Cannan, ed. (Oxford, 1896), p. 75.

7. Millar, *op. cit.*, pp. 65–6. Millar says, "Rude nations are usually distinguished" by "plainness of behaviour." *Idem*, p. 30. Later Millar observes that "in all barbarous countries" the old men are respected for wisdom. This was true in Greece and it was true in Scotland in Ossian's time. *Idem*, p. 109.

8. *Idem*, p. 143.

hommes sont avides de merveilleux." He therefore filled his "histories" with amazing stories about monsters and gods.[9] Having observed that all barbarous nations have their heroic poems—some of which are transcribed, while others are handed down from father to son— Priestley says that the epics of Homer, and especially the *Iliad*, "bear evident marks of their being founded on fact, notwithstanding the mixture of the absurd Grecian mythology with them."[1] Though the original story might undergo some alterations in the hands of the poet, its "circumstantial" nature and the "remarkable distinctness" of many of its characters would suggest that there had been little variation of essential facts.[2] Agreeing with these opinions, another critic says that "the *marvellous* in Homer, has in too great a measure, weakened his credit as an historian."[3] The Greek poet has often represented the Trojan heroes in a more amiable light than his own countrymen, he says, and this fact gives us some reason to suppose that "there is more true history" in Homer's epics than we might imagine,[4] that the narratives were based upon actual events and graced with the marvelous in order to "exalt an history into a poem."[5] This was substantially the argument of another writer. Because Homer had so great a respect for truth and because he was personally acquainted with the descendants of the house of Priam, he felt obliged to depict Hector as a more likable individual than his real hero, Achilles. One's opinion of the *Iliad* suffers, therefore; but it must be remembered that such a defect is not "justly chargeable on Homer."[6]

That Homer had attempted to please his contemporaries, Greek and Trojan, seems to have been a point that was repeatedly stressed.[7] The catalogue of ships in the *Iliad* and the many long speeches giving the genealogies of warriors were often considered as evidence that the poet was trying to win the favor of his readers. In an anonymous essay published in 1739, the author observes how the various nations

9. "Plan du second discours sur l'histoire universelle, dont l'objet sera les progrès de l'esprit humain," in *Oeuvres de Turgot,* Dupont de Nemours, Eugène Daire, and *Hippolyte Dussard,* eds. (Paris, 1844), II, 649. Turgot's "plan" was first jotted down about 1750.

1. Joseph Priestley, *Lectures on History, and General Policy: to Which Is Prefixed, an Essay on a Course of Liberal Education for Civil and Active Life* (Dublin, 1791), pp. 42–3. In a dedication to Benjamin Vaughan, dated January 1, 1788, Priestley reminds his former pupil that these lectures had been delivered many years before their publication.

2. *Idem,* p. 43.   3. John Armstrong, *Miscellanies* (London, 1770), II, 219.
4. *Idem,* II, 219–20.   5. *Idem,* II, 220.
6. Duff, *op. cit.,* pp. 17–18.

7. One suspects, though one cannot prove, that William Wilkie's discussion of "historical circumstances" in Homer (preface to the *Epigoniad*) strongly influenced many Homeric critics, at least after the middle of the century.

were represented in the *Iliad*,[8] how the people of each country could find descriptions of their native land,[9] and how the names of Homer's acquaintances were sometimes inserted in the two epics. Themius, he says, was the poet's schoolmaster, and Mentor was given "a very honourable Post" in the *Odyssey* because he was a well-known sage and patron of the day.[1] Shenstone says that the ancient poets were proud of "perpetuating the fame of their cotemporaries";[2] and Voltaire says that Homer had a higher reputation than Hesiod because he wrote about a war "la plus mémorable du premier peuple de l'Europe" and because he celebrated the reigning houses of his own time.[3]

One may ask whether comments of this kind had any effect upon the criticism of Homer. I believe that they had a very profound effect. Above all, they discouraged further the earlier view that Homer's poems were timeless creations, were works to be read without much consideration of the social circumstances influencing the nature of these poems. Instead of attributing everything to the poetic genius of an individual named Homer, these writers began with the assumption that there were external causes for the peculiar characteristics of the *Iliad* and *Odyssey*. Heroic manners, customs, even the events themselves, could be studied historically, could be accepted as indications of the way men lived in early times, because it was believed that Homer had not been an inventor, that, even if he had had the genius to make history poetical, the materials for his "history" were not really his own. Though this group of critics may have been more interested in the society than in the literary productions of that society, this assumption and the analyses of the poems based upon it could scarcely escape those whose interests were mainly literary. They could not avoid having thrust upon them the realization that Homer's epics belong to a definite time and place and that the individualities of his poetry are seemingly more in evidence than the so-called universal qualities. It was certainly no longer possible to believe that anything was superficial, that the historian should concern himself with social backgrounds, while the literary critic discussed matters of a very different kind. Criticism and history were close together and it became harder and harder to separate the two fields.

Growing out of this tendency to turn to Homer as a historian was

8. "A Discourse on Ancient and Modern Learning," in *The Miscellaneous Works of Joseph Addison*, A. C. Guthkelch, ed. (London, 1914), II, 457. (The editor attributes the "Discourse" to Addison.)

9. *Idem*, II, 450.   1. *Ibid*.

2. "Essays on Men and Manners," in *The Works in Verse and Prose, of William Shenstone, Esq.* (London, 1768), II, 170.

3. "Dictionnaire Philosophique," in *Oeuvres complètes de Voltaire*, XVIII, 566.

another tendency with important bearings upon future Homeric criticism. Instead of maintaining that the Greek bard had appeared before poetry had made any appreciable advance and that he had suddenly brought the epic to its highest point of development, some of the French and English writers began to consider Homer as the last and most important member of a long procession of inspired poets.[4] For instance, Warburton declares that Homer had not merely used oral traditions concerning the Trojan War but that he was also "possessed of the Songs and Poems of his ancestors; in which he found all the particulars of that famous expedition."[5] Again, Warburton says that the poet used "authentic records," particularly in constructing the catalogue of Greek forces which participated in the war.[6] Though the *Iliad* and *Odyssey* were widely acclaimed by the ancients, they received those acclamations because they had "so greatly eclipsed" all the earlier poems and not because Homer had written anything new or different.[7] Millot points out, even as Beattie and Walpole did,[8] that there is every reason for believing that other bards preceded Homer, for poetry, as a spontaneous expression of passion, is "cultivated in all savage nations" at an early date.[9] While he did not subscribe to the opinion, Melmoth observes that some critics pretend that "even Homer himself was indebted to the antients," that his "full streams" flowed from a higher source;[1] and Lauder notes that Homer, as well as Virgil and the later writers, "is accused of borrowing largely from his Predecessors."[2] As we have already said, John Brown believed that there were many poets before Homer, some of whom sang about the Trojan horse and the re-

4. This theory had at least been suggested by William Temple and possibly by a few other authors of the late seventeenth century but it had not seemed particularly significant to them.

5. Warburton, *op. cit.*, III, 308.

6. *Idem*, III, 308, n. This catalogue, Warburton says, was "the likeliest of all subjects to be found in the old poems of his Ancestors."

7. *Idem*, III, 60.

8. Walpole observes that "the poetry of Homer is a sufficient proof that there were poets of eminence before him; for no language can leap from its infancy at once to perfection, and the Greek shines with its brightest lustre in his works." Horace Walpole, *Anecdotes of Polite Literature* (London, 1764), I, 61. In a letter to Lord Kames, dated February, 1762, James Harris says: "had not Linus, Musaeus, and those other songsters, which the old bard himself mentions, existed *before*, there had never, I fancy, been Homer." Tytler, *Memoirs of the Life and Writings of the Honourable Henry Home of Kames*, II, 9. For other opinions on this subject, see James Harris, *Hermes, or a Philosophical Inquiry Concerning Universal Grammar* (London, 1794), II, 417, n.; "Of Memory and Imagination," in Beattie, *op. cit.*, I, 231.

9. Millot, *op. cit.*, I, 363.

1. William Melmoth, *The Letters of Sir Thomas Fitzosborne, on Several Subjects* (London, 1784), p. 21.

2. William Lauder, *An Essay upon Milton's Imitations of the Ancients in His Paradise Lost. With Some Observations on the Paradise Regain'd* (—, 1741), p. 47.

turn of the Greeks with Agamemnon.[3] Finally, to conclude this list of authorities, Marmontel goes back even further, discovering "qu'avant Homère et avant les poëtes qui l'avaient précédé, il y avait eu de ces *trouvères*" who composed poems and songs which were known to the later bards and were joined into well-ordered narratives by them.[4]

Closely connected with arguments of this kind was the traditional belief that the writings of Homer had not been organized into two unified epics until some time after the poet's death. According to John Harvey, the "materials for the Iliad," instead of being divided into books, "were originally sung or recited in little broken sketches, then called by the Greeks *rhapsodies*," by which name they were known until Lycurgus collected them "into some form" and until in the time of Solon they were "digested" into the order in which we now have them.[5] Newberry is of the opinion that the various books of the *Iliad* "seem in a manner detached, and are so independent" that many could be transposed without affecting the progress of the epic action. Perhaps for that reason they were given the name "Rhapsodies," he adds.[6] To Dr. Johnson, Ramsay once made a startling remark: " 'I suppose Homer's *Iliad* to be a collection of pieces which had been written before his time.' "[7] In another conversation reported by Boswell, Macqueen told Johnson that "Homer was made up of detached fragments. Mr. Johnson denied it; said that it had been one work originally, and that you could not put a book of the *Iliad* out of its place."[8] The same was true of the *Odyssey*, he thought.

Criticism of this type was obviously capable of giving added support to the Pisistratus theory which had been discussed earlier in the century, a theory which was by no means unknown to the writers we have been considering.[9] If it was granted that other poets had pre-

---

3. See Brown, *op. cit.*, pp. 102–05.

4. "Essai sur les Romans," in *Oeuvres complètes de Marmontel* (Paris, 1819), x, 290–1.

5. John Harvey, *The Bruciad, an Epic Poem, in Six Books* (London, 1769), pp. xii–xiii.

6. Newberry, *op. cit.*, ii, 226. Newberry speaks of the early Greek, Roman, and British bards, who "made songs in praise of their heroes, which they adapted to music, and sung to their harps." *Idem*, i, iv (Introduction).

7. *Boswell's Life of Johnson*, G. B. Hill, ed. (Oxford and New York, 1887), iii, 333.

8. Pottle and Bennett, *op. cit.*, p. 129.

9. Husbands says that "LYCURGUS was so great a Friend to the Muses, that he digested into order the Works of *Homer*." Husbands, *op. cit.*, Preface. Voltaire observes that, even after the time of Lycurgus, Homer's poems "furent longtemps si peu connus" that Pisistratus had them transcribed anew. "Dictionnaire philosophique," in *Oeuvres complètes de Voltaire*, xix, 595. Batteux states that one finds in the *Iliad* "le même style, le même génie," and it therefore seems certain that we have the poems of Homer as they were originally written. Charles Batteux, "Du Poème épique," in *Principes de la littérature* (Avignon, 1809), ii, 262.

ceded Homer and that he had not suddenly brought the epic to its full perfection, was it not at least possible that the poems ascribed to him were compilations of the songs of rhapsodists? Might not these songs have been collected by Homer or, if a man named Homer never existed, by someone else? Questions like these were not asked at this time, of course. But it is easy to see how, with a little more knowledge about early poetry and early societies and perhaps with a little more imagination, someone might eventually be led to ask them.

An equally significant contribution of the eighteenth-century critics was the conception of Homer as a kind of balladist or inspired singer. For example, Bielfeld says that the Greek poet "sung his *Iliad* and *Odyssey* for charity, as he went begging through the cities of Greece";[1] and Pinkerton, though he concedes that Homer might "have been a petty king just as likely as a beggar," gives him the dubious distinction of being the only bard of antiquity who was poor.[2] In the *Citizen of the World,* Goldsmith observes that "Homer is the first poet and beggar of note among the ancients: he was blind, and sung his ballads about the streets"; and "his mouth was more frequently filled with verses than with bread."[3] After speaking of the small monetary rewards which Blackwell received for his book, Mrs. Montagu adds that "Homer, though hungry, thirsty, and a beggar, can feed his heroes and kings with whole bulls and heifers," and give them drink out of sculptured vases, and allow them costly carpets to sleep upon, "while himself continued to lodge perhaps on the ground!"[4] Bolingbroke states that the poets before Homer sang their "canticles, philosophical rhapsodies, and heroical ballads," as it is reported "that he did after them."[5] In the preface to his *Warbling Muses,* Wakefield asserts that songs are "the Delight" of all people in all ages and that in early times "they served as the first Records" to transmit great events to posterity. "Historians tell us," he says, "that the several Parts of *Homer's Iliad* were sung in this manner."[6] A facetious writer in the *World* says that the invention of the ballad could probably be attributed "to old Homer himself, who hawked his

1. Jacques Frédéric, Baron de Bielfeld, *The Elements of Universal Erudition, Containing an Analytical Abridgment of the Sciences, Polite Arts, and Belles Lettres,* W. Hooper, tr. (London, 1770), II, 203.

2. Pinkerton, *Letters of Literature,* p. 76.

3. *The Works of Oliver Goldsmith,* J. W. M. Gibbs, ed. (London, 1884), III, 314.

4. *The Letters of Mrs. Montagu, with Some of the Letters of Her Correspondents,* Mathew Montagu, publisher (London, 1809–13). Mrs. Montagu makes these observations in a letter to the Duchess of Portland, October 11 (1741).

5. "On the Propagation of Errour and Superstition," in *The Works of the Late Right Honourable Henry St. John, Lord Viscount Bolingbroke* (London, 1809), VI, 9.

6. Benjamin Wakefield, *The Warbling Muses, or Treasure of Lyric Poetry* (London, 1749), pp. x–xi.

Iliad about the streets for an obolus a book." Because there was no demand for the ballad in those days and because his poetry was crude, "he could scarce earn bread for himself and his family."[7] Writing to Thomas Warton in May, 1761, Percy said that "the old Songs about King Arthur and his Knights, seem to have been as current among our plain, but martial, Ancestors as the *Rhapsodies* of Homer were among his countrymen."[8] Even the Greek heroes, such as Achilles, Ajax, Agamemnon, and Thersites, were not more familiar to the ancients than Arthur, Kay, Guinevere, and Gawain were to medieval Europe. The traveller, Joseph Banks, observes that the natives of the South Seas "sang many songs, generally in praise of us, for these gentlemen, like Homer of old, must be poets as well as musicians."[9] Finally, on the assumption that *Hardyknute* was a part of an epic poem, one daring critic went so far as to compare that ballad with the *Iliad*. Its author had "a large Portion of the fiery Spirit of *Homer*," he says,[1] and there are the same digressions, the same use of similes, and the same ferocious heroes.[2]

Strengthening the theory that Homer was an inspired songster was the new emphasis placed upon the marvelous and romantic nature of the *Iliad* and *Odyssey* and the Greek poet's enthusiasm and great powers of imagination. Thus, in referring to Homer, Hurd says that in the "*simpler ages of learning*" each writer with a "vehement and impetuous genius" puts down his "*first thoughts*" in the most elementary words of the language he uses.[3] According to Mrs. Montagu, the Welsh bards "appear to be the natural sons of Homer," inheriting "his spirit" and having "more of his fire" than the later Greek and Roman poets.[4] Observing that "the oldest Poets" usually have the

7. Chalmers, *op. cit.*, XXVIII, 232–3 (*World*, No. 149, November 6, 1755).
8. Leah Dennis, "The Text of the Percy-Warton Letters," *PMLA*, XLVI (1931), 1169. Ramsay sent one of his early collections of songs and ballads into the world with the words, "*Now, Little Books, go your ways; . . . you are to live too as long as the Song of Homer in Greek and English.*" Allan Ramsay, *The Tea-Table Miscellany: Or, a Complete Collection of Scots Songs* (Dublin, 1729), p. viii.
9. *Journal of the Right Hon. Sir Joseph Banks, Bart., K.B., P.R.S. during Captain Cook's First Voyage in H.M.S. "Endeavour" in 1768–71 to Terra del Fuego, Otahite, New Zealand, Australia, the Dutch East Indies, Etc.*, J. D. Hooker, ed. (London, 1896), p. 99. Entry for June 12, 1769.
1. E. Wardlaw, *Hardyknute: A Fragment. Being the First Canto of an Epick Poem; with General Remarks, and Notes* (London, 1740), p. 7.
2. The author says: "Hector . . . does not wear a more dreadful Appearance than *Hardyknute*, upon his only hearing, as it were, the distant Sound of Arms." *Idem*, p. 15, n. It might be added that the tendency to call the epic a heroic ballad, and the heroic ballad an epic, encouraged such comparisons as this. See Reeve, *op. cit.*, I, 21; and the discussion of the heroic ballad in John Aikin, "An Essay on Ballads and Pastoral Songs," in *Essays on Song-Writing: with a Collection of Such English Songs as Are Most Eminent for Poetical Merit* (Warrington, 1774), pp. 26–7.
3. "Notes on the Epistle to Augustus," in *Q. Horatii Flacci Epistolae*, I, 267.
4. *Letters of Mrs. Montagu*, IV, 112. To Benjamin Stillingfleet, October 22, 1758.

greatest enthusiasm and the least amount of art, John Campbell states that it is to "nature" that Homer owes his superiority. In "the Rapidity of his Numbers, and the wonderful Strength of his Genius he is justly stiled inimitable."[5] The sublime Cædmon, he adds, was "the *Saxon Homer*," endowed with the *"Furor Poeticus"* and the *"Divine Rage"* of the early poet.[6] Again and again, one finds the mid-eighteenth-century critic ignoring the bard's knowledge of art and speaking rapturously of Homer as an early singer, with his "imagination riche et brillante," his "enthousiasme presque divin," and his "si grande énergie."[7]

One might expect that there was nothing to prompt a development of Homeric criticism similar to that in Scotland. There was no English primitivist movement in which Homer would probably be made a central figure. There was no favorite bard of early date, like Ossian, with whom to compare him nor an English Blackwell to draw attention to early Greek literature. But a movement was under way in England which was far wider in scope than primitivism and which involved Homer at least as much. Critics were applying the historical approach to poets of all times and all nations, sometimes only to explain, often to "prove" the superiority of one poet over others. Hence, while one critic spoke of the Trojan War as history, another discussed the rise of feudalism and its effect upon Spenser. While one dealt with Homer's use of gods, another was defending Shakespeare's use of ghosts and witches. It is true, of course, that many Homeric critics were progressivists, historians, and pedants, without the breadth of view of a man like Thomas Warton and often without any particular appreciation of literature. But with few exceptions most of those who criticized the English poets were of the same type. Their work was often superficial, their editing was hopelessly inadequate, their treatments of influences of one author upon another were full of guesswork, and their interests were often nonliterary. In all fairness to these critics of Homer and of the English poets, one must recognize that the historical approach is a good deal more complex than the neoclassical one, requiring a good deal more knowledge on the part of those who use it. Also, because of its complexity, it can be and usually has been applied in all kinds of ways by all kinds of persons. One could hardly expect, in its first stages of development, that the new approach should be used by competent scholars merely to help understand and perhaps criticize more intelligently or that there should be the relativity of historical criticism.

5. John Campbell, *The Rational Amusement: Comprehending a Collection of Letters on a Great Variety of Subjects, Serious, Entertaining, Moral, Diverting, and Instructive* (London, 1754), pp. 246–7.

6. *Idem*, p. 263.   7. Batteux, *op. cit.*, II, 263.

One other thing links Homeric criticism with criticism of English poets. In that day when scholars and critics were not specialists there was less inclination than now to limit oneself to study of a single author or one nation's literature. It was not usual to write only of Homer or even of Greek poetry. Richard Hurd, for example, went so far as to use the historical approach in comparing Homer and Spenser. Others were fond of making distinctions between Homer and Virgil or perhaps Homer and the Bible. And a still larger group, without making actual comparisons, had equally important things to say about Homer and the English poets. As we have seen, this was true of Mrs. Montagu and it was even more true of Joseph Warton. Homeric criticism, broadly speaking, was not only linked with criticism of English authors but a part of the whole historical movement.

One cannot deny, of course, that there were some very specific differences in the treatments of Homer and Spenser, even if these general likenesses do exist. When the historical approach was made to Spenser, the main purpose seems to have been to encourage something like relativist criticism of that author, to give him his rightful place as a great poet. When the same approach was made to Homer, there was almost never any thought of relativist criticism. The critic's object, as before, was to "prove" either of two things: that Homer and the ancients were the greatest poets or that they were the least valuable of all poets to modern readers. It was still the age-old controversy over progress, literary and social, and Homer was still a major figure in it. But, unfortunately for those who admired everything Greek, English nationalistic spirit was only adding to their difficulties. Greater interest in England's past was leading to a definite prejudice in favor of native poets, no matter how obscure, and it was becoming harder and harder to convince an Englishman that Homer should mean as much to him as Spenser or Milton or the early ballads. Everything was forgotten because of this new enthusiasm—Homer's timeless qualities, his high reputation throughout the ages, practically everything except his influence upon English literature. He was dismissed, usually in a few words, as a barbarian.

In general procedure there were also some differences between the critics of Homer and the critics of English poets. For example, the predecessors of Homer being unknown, there being few reliable accounts of early Greek history, one was confined almost entirely to a study of Homer's poems themselves. He was able to say merely that Homer probably knew the writings of Orpheus, Musaeus, and Linus and histories of the Trojan War no longer extant. Those who criticized Spenser or Milton, on the other hand, had an abundance of primary sources with which to work, historical and literary. They could and did speak of Spenser's indebtedness to other Elizabethans,

to Chaucer, to the Italians, and to the classical poets. But such differences in method obviously were not of the critic's choosing: the available materials dictated the manner of approach.

In considering Homeric criticism apart, it becomes apparent at
once that the fields of literature and history were overlapping each
other as never before—to a far greater degree than in the treatments
of most English poets. Because of the emphasis upon backgrounds
and because Homer had obviously related a semihistorical account of
Troy, it was natural that the *Iliad* should often be regarded as a docu-
ment rather than a poem. Historians and critics alike were constantly
saying that the first histories had been in verse, and the first verse
usually dealt with political events in a mythological setting. In fact,
the term "epic" came to mean, by degrees, an imaginative record of
heroic deeds. With speculation running high as to the relation of fact
and fiction in Homer's poetry, there was a great deal of preoccupation
with detached bits of historical data, a tendency to seek and interpret
out-of-the-way facts overlooked in the past. There were discussions,
short and long, of the sort that were to lead to explanations of a single
figure on Achilles' shield or of the historical importance of a divinity
mentioned in a line of Homer. There were books, usually by historians, full of references to customs and habits described in the
Odyssey and in most early poetry, and every history of Greece contained a chapter or two dealing with Homer's account of Troy.

Encouraged no doubt by the historian's use of literature in studying the past, the critic had become so deeply interested in facts in
literature that it is sometimes not easy to distinguish him from the
historian. Thomas Warton, for instance, derived much of his pleasure
in reading Homer from being able to trace man's "transition from
barbarity to civility." Richard Hurd singled out for special praise the
figures and descriptions in Homer which had been derived from every
art "invented for the service or ornament of society." As a rule, however, the critic was not concerned with a fact per se or as a means of
filling in gaps in history. He wished to find a way of discriminating
between poems, of differentiating between the good and bad ones.
Since he had little faith in the absolute values of formal criticism, his
task, it seemed, was to examine the "content" of a particular poem, to
arrive at some conclusion about its value to the present world, and
so to decide whether that poem deserved praise or censure. Hence
some talked longingly about the simplicity of the Homeric Greek;
others, content with their own age, railed at the barbarous deeds
related by Homer and said his poems were worthless.

As shown by these opposing views and the many views midway between, the historical approach was creating a temporary state of
chaos—in Homeric criticism, at least. The term "epic" could now

mean almost anything, especially since form had ceased to be an important means of determining to which literary genre a poem belonged. The emphasis upon content had led to the assumption that, as it was indicated earlier, an epic was any poetic account of mighty actions, half historical, half fictitious—actions of national heroes who were human and divine at the same time and were surrounded by hosts of supernatural beings such as gods, ghosts, and giants. As an epic poet, therefore, Homer began to have strange competitors from all parts of the world. But it was also believed that many of the so-called epics had a great deal in common with the romance, Oriental, French, and English. There were often similar narrations of heroic deeds, elaborated until they had become superhuman. There was the same use of "machinery"—strange beings who directed the affairs of mankind. Since the dividing line between these two genres was so shadowy, it seemed perfectly logical to some critics to think of Homer as a writer of romances. Mrs. Reeve, for example, pointed out that Odysseus' voyages were like the travels of Sindbad the Sailor: both had met with exciting and unbelievable adventures. Also, it was possible to regard the early epic as a kind of ballad. *Chevy Chase,* as Addison once said, had something in common with the *Iliad,* each poem being a record of stirring events in the history of a people. A later critic compared *Hardyknute* with the *Iliad* and Ramsay suggested that Homer's poems could have been collections of early folktales.

To what these discussions were leading it would soon become clear. In general, one can say that, because the relation of Homer to the modern world was not so close as it once seemed, there was virtually no way to regard him except as an inspired poet of the dim and distant past. More specifically, the emphasis upon fact was to make Homer a special and permanent interest to historians and to scholars. If a distinction between the two is allowed, one may say that the former were to make Homer a primary source for every student of Greek history, while the latter, assuming that nothing is too insignificant to explain, would find endless subjects in Homer to investigate or clarify. The bitter controversy over Homer in the following century is well known—the strife stirred up by the scholarly work of Heyne and especially Wolf, the countless attempts to explain the origin of Homer's poems. Literary critics had fought over Homer a hundred years earlier, using history as a means of evaluating his poetry. Now it was the turn of the scholar, expert and amateur, to use the historical approach to dissect him once again and to find out whether a Homer ever existed.

While the German critics of the nineteenth century took sides in this quarrel, the English were not generally inclined to wrangle about the authorship of the Homeric poems. On the whole, their task was to carry forward the new view of Homer's epics as compositions of a primitive poet and now, seemingly for the first time, to point out why he should be regarded as a genius in his own right. There was no need, they said, to go to one extreme or the other—to idealize or scorn Homer on the basis of one's estimate of Greek society. Nor ought the existence of a particular English poet to affect the value of any other poet, English or Greek. Since the *Iliad* and the *Faerie Queene* had been affected, even "formed," by different environments and different personal experiences, it was necessary to use different criteria in estimating them. Relative rather than absolute standards were to be applied, and historical criticism—judgment of poetry as an "expression of an age"—was to follow the historical perspective of the eighteenth century.

VI

Robert Wood and German Criticism

IN September, 1775, there appeared in the *Critical Review* a discussion of a study of Homer which had just come before the attention of the English public. Glancing back some forty years, the critic observed that in his *Enquiry* Thomas Blackwell had attempted to show that "a concourse of natural causes" was responsible for the *Iliad* and *Odyssey,* that the climate, politics, and manners of Greece had given the poet a marked advantage over the later authors of his own country and of Rome. "But having never seen the great theatre of action, the fields of Troy, nor any of the places, which are mentioned by Homer, he has of course left many circumstances for the investigation of succeeding writers."[1] Such an investigation, the reviewer declares, had been made by Robert Wood, a scholar who had travelled in Greece and Asia Minor, had read the two epics in the places which they described, had seen such communities as those among which Homer had sung his compositions, the plain where Achilles fought, and the lands which Ulysses visited; and who, upon his return home, had given an account of his discoveries in his *Essay upon the Original Genius and Writings of Homer.*

One might well wish to question this reviewer and those who agreed with him to find out why a traveller was thought to have an advantage over the experienced critic who had never been out of England or over any man of letters who might offer his observations on the Homeric poems after reading them attentively. Now, several answers would probably be given. In the first place, it was believed that one who had not visited the scene of action of the *Iliad* and *Odyssey* was in no position to understand or to appreciate fully the minute descriptions found throughout those poems. Long before Wood made his trip, Lady Mary Wortley Montagu had journeyed through this region with a copy of the epics in her hand, had viewed the "celebrated fields and rivers" of Troy, and had admired "the exact geography of Homer." With enthusiasm she wrote a friend that "almost every epithet he gives to a mountain or plain is still just for it; and I spent several hours in as agreeable cogitations as ever Don Quixote had on mount Montesinos."[2] In the same letter Lady Mary

1. *Critical Review,* XL (September, 1775), 171.
2. *The Letters and Works of Lady Mary Wortley Montagu,* Lord Wharncliffe and W. Moy Thomas, eds. (London, 1887), II, 253. Letter to the Abbé Conti, July 31 (1718) O. S.

Montagu speaks of the pleasure she experienced in sailing along the coast of Italy, observing that she neither heard Homer's sirens nor was endangered by Scylla and Charybdis.[3] Similarly, another writer remarked that it is necessary to read Homer and the later Greek poets in their native land "pour faire attention aux plus petits détails qu'ils présentent, parce qu'on les a sous les yeux, & qu'on est bien aise de les retrouver."[4] Pleased at having been able to read the *Iliad* on the site of ancient Troy, he exclaims: "Quelle vérité! quelle énergie! quel choix dans toutes ses images!"[5]

But it was not merely in order to observe the poet's fidelity to "nature" that one should visit Greece with a volume of Homer in his hand. For one or two critics also believed that it was essential to know the natural objects—the clear sky, the fertile fields, and the rugged aspects of the country—which had been factors "le plus propre à développer, à étendre encore & à aggrandir le génie."[6] Remembering that Addison, Dubos, and Blackwell had so strongly emphasized the effects of environment upon poetic creations, it is perhaps not surprising that Guys should think it advisable to study at first hand the climate and physical features which had done so much to advance the genius of Homer and the later bards. Finally, something was to be gained by noting how the people of modern Greece lived, for in many sections of that country the manners and customs of Homer's contemporaries were still preserved. An observant traveller could thus compare the habits and modes of behavior of Alcinous, Nausicaa, and Ulysses with those he found at the present time and could perhaps shed new light upon the way in which the poet had represented the heroes of antiquity. As a matter of fact, a large part of Guys's book is devoted to a discussion of the similarities between the customs and occupations of the ancient and modern Greeks, between their domestic duties, their attitudes toward the relationship of the sexes, etc.

Development of the historical approach was not, of course, directly responsible for comments or analyses of this sort. Particularly after 1732, the year in which the Society of Dilettanti was founded, there seems to have been a steadily growing interest in classical archeology and, perhaps as a result, in the societies of eastern Europe and Asia Minor, both past and present. For example, Richard Pococke in 1737 began a journey which took him to Egypt, Palestine, parts of Asia Minor, and Greece. In 1751 James Stuart and Nicholas Revett made a

---

3. *Idem,* II, 256–7.   4. Guys, *Voyage littéraire de la Grèce,* I, 58.
5. *Idem,* I, 518–19. He adds, "C'est en Grèce qu'il faut relire l'Iliade & l'Odyssée." *Idem,* I, 519. Addison speaks of the "great Pleasure" experienced by Homer's audiences, which "had every Day perhaps in their Sight the Mountain or Field where such an Adventure happen'd, or such a Battle was fought." "A Discourse on Ancient and Modern Learning," in *The Miscellaneous Works of Joseph Addison,* Guthkelch, ed., II, 455.
6. Guys, *op. cit.,* I, 474.

similar expedition, publishing some years later the fruit of their research, *The Antiquities of Athens*. Also in 1751 Robert Wood and James Dawkins arrived in Athens on the first leg of a trip which eventually included a large part of Greece and Asia Minor. The results of their study are discussed in *The Ruins of Palmyra* (1753), *The Ruins of Balbec* (1757), and the book on Homer which will be considered in some detail in this chapter. Another famous traveller was Richard Chandler, who left England in 1764 with Revett and William Pars on a journey to Greece and neighboring countries. *Ionian Antiquities*, sponsored by the Society of Dilettanti, was published in 1769 after Chandler's return.

As Bernard Stern has shown, there is definite evidence of romantic Hellenism in the writings of these travellers.[7] They seem to have a sentimental admiration for the scenery and for the inhabitants of modern Greece, they rail at the Turks for the destruction of Greek architecture, and they lament the decay, long ago, of Greek culture, government, and love of liberty. In dealing with antiquity, it is of course apparent that most of these writers were concerned with the Greece of Phidias and Praxiteles—with the greatest period of Greek art rather than with the age of Homer. Hence, until archeological investigations began to center around Troy and even for some time afterward, there was not much occasion to speak of Homer or to idealize the time in which he lived. Of the mid-eighteenth-century travellers, in fact, Wood alone seems to have made thorough investigations in the region of Troy and he alone associates Homer with the glory that was Greece.

Because of his position as undersecretary to Pitt (1756–63) and his various activities in the Society of Dilettanti, Wood was unable to publish an account of his travels until 1767. In its original form the book was entitled *A Comparative View of the Antient and Present State of the Troade. To Which Is Prefixed an Essay on the Original Genius of Homer*. An enlarged edition of *An Essay on the Original Genius of Homer* appeared in 1769. Even then the book was left incomplete and no more than half a dozen copies were published. Though Wood's friends kept insisting that he print a large edition for the English public, nothing further was done and, when the author died in 1771, the unfinished *Essay* was left in his wife's possession. A search was then begun in order to find someone who would arrange for a new publication of the work. Requested to undertake the task, Jacob Bryant pleaded that he was much too busy with his own scholarly endeavors and urged that someone else be selected.[8] However, three years later (1775) Bryant wrote to J. D. Michaelis,

7. See Bernard Stern, *The Rise of Romantic Hellenism* (Menasha, Wis., 1940).
8. *Literarischer Briefwechsel von Johann David Michaelis*, J. G. Buhle, ed. (Leipzig, 1794), III, 208–09. Letter from Bryant to Michaelis, December 10, 1772.

the German antiquarian, saying that he had revised Wood's *Essay* and was now forwarding a copy of the new edition.[9] Thus nearly a quarter of a century elapsed before the work which was to prove the most important single contribution to Homeric criticism between Blackwell and Wolf finally appeared before the public. Everywhere, on the Continent and in England, its success was immediately proclaimed[1] and there were many expressions of regret that Wood had not lived, both to receive his due recognition and to expand the somewhat sketchy text.

What, then, was the primary purpose of the *Essay* on Homer? Did the author intend to render anything more than a pedantic account of his travels in Asia Minor and Greece? Judging from the types of subjects discussed, he apparently had no thought of repeating what had already been so thoroughly treated by Blackwell; and, when some of the problems of the *Enquiry* were occasionally raised, he at least had new information to offer toward their solution.[2] Wood did not conjecture why Homer had been the greatest poet in three thousand years. Instead, his primary purpose was to prove how exactly the bard had described the lands of the Greeks and Trojans and how exactly he had represented the characters of men of both nations. Having surveyed most of Greece and Asia Minor, and their towns, rivers, and mountains, and having studied the manners and customs of Eastern countries, Wood hoped to provide a better commentary upon Homer's poems than had been given by those critics who drew their conclusions from the epics themselves, or from some ancient history, or from an inadequate and bookish knowledge of primitive societies in general. To examine Homer in relation to his age was not enough: to understand his "peculiar precision" and exactness in portraying manners and landscapes,[3] it was necessary for the critic to "approach his country and age."[4]

With the plan of illustrating Homer's faithful descriptions of places

9. *Idem*, II, 506. Letter dated June 28, 1775.

1. See *Gentleman's Magazine*, XLV (October, 1775), 483–7. The only hostile criticism appeared in an article entitled "An Examination of Mr. Wood's Essay Concerning the Genius of Homer," in *Critical Observations on Books, Antient and Modern* (London, 1776), I.

2. When Wood mentions the *Enquiry*, he does so only to challenge some point set forth by Blackwell.

3. Robert Wood, *An Essay on the Original Genius and Writings of Homer: with a Comparative View of the Ancient and Present State of the Troade* (London, 1775), p. xii. All quotations have been taken from the rare quarto edition of 1775, which must be distinguished from the octavo edition of the same year.

4. *Idem*, p. vi. Wood says "we should approach, as near as possible, to the time and place, when and where, he wrote." *Idem*, p. ix. This is especially desirable in studying the *Odyssey*, for "its beauties are more local, and its paintings are often of that finished kind, which produces resemblance and character out of very trivial incidents; and these delicate touches . . . are so minute, as to escape observation, if the copy and the original be not confronted." *Idem*, pp. ix–x.

and men, Wood thus opened his investigation by examining the materials of the *Iliad* and *Odyssey* "not only where they were collected, but, as nearly as possible, in the same order, in the same light, and under the same point of view, in which I imagine they presented themselves to the Poet's choice."[5] He tried to determine where Homer had been born and bred not by using the information of Greek and Roman authorities but by comparing the poet's descriptions with the true nature of countries in that neighborhood. Believing that a "curious and attentive observer of Nature is perhaps most liable to retain those marks of locality,"[6] Wood carefully analyzes the similes of the two epics and finds that the majority of them were drawn from the natural phenomena and the physical features of Ionia. He finds, for example, that Homer is the only Greek or Roman poet to give the zephyr "that rough character, so little known to western climates" and so commonly associated with Ionia[7]—a character given it when the poet compares the clashing of warriors to a storm rising out of the west.[8] As additional evidence that this was Homer's native land, Wood points out that Ionia is the only place which is not described with the circumstantiality of the traveller.[9]

Wood then devotes nearly two chapters to a consideration of Homer's journeys, using his own first-hand knowledge of the entire region instead of making conjectures as Blackwell had done. Wherever Menelaus or Ulysses had gone by sea, there Wood had also been. If it had taken the heroes five days to accomplish a certain trip, Wood found that it took him exactly the same length of time. If the heroes did not follow the most direct course, Wood tried to discover why—whether there were hidden rocks or whether the type of vessel used in ancient times was unable to stand the battering seas and strong winds. If a distant view of an island was said to be purple or blue, he found that that was the general impression it gave when seen from a certain point of vantage.

Wood next speaks of the contrast between the accuracy of the original *Iliad* and the various English and French translations of that poem. In Homer, he says, every description of "rock, hill, dale," every "shady grove, verdant lawn, and flowery mead" affords "unquestionable testimony" of the poet's "correctness."[1] In Pope, on the other

5. *Idem*, p. 5.   6. *Idem*, p. 21.
7. *Idem*, p. 24. Also see pp. 28–9.
8. Speaking of the storms which might be seen from the Ionian coast, Wood says that the poet "recalls the images, that a particular striking appearance of Nature had strongly impressed upon his youthful fancy, retaining the same local associations, which accompanied his first warm conception of them." *Idem*, p. 20.
9. *Idem*, p. 30.
1. *Idem*, p. 75. Wood remarks that, considering how greatly both the Eastern countries and Homer's poems have been altered, "his descriptions correspond more with present appearances, than could be reasonably expected." *Idem*, pp. 74–5.

hand, the use of rhyme, a desire to ornament the *Iliad*, and an unwillingness to translate literally have produced a strangely confused picture of ancient Greece, of its geography as well as its manners.[2] As a
crowning example of the Englishman's inexactitude, Wood calls attention to the passage in Pope in which Achilles is one moment said
to be sleeping upon the rocky shore, the next upon the soft grass, and
later to be arising from the sands. "Should we give this sleepy Achilles
to a painter, he must be strangely puzzled with the hero's rocky,
grassy, sandy couch."[3]

Was Wood nothing more than a quibbling pedant in showing such
concern about the most insignificant details of Homer? Why should
it matter whether a wind came from the east, or a certain island appeared in the southwest, or it took Ulysses six days to go from one
place to another? Now, it is, of course, true that the critic who used
a historical approach, rather than the neoclassicist, had some reason
to be interested in the closeness with which a poet followed his
original. If he intended to defend or to explain the poet's practice, if
he wished to show that a work of art reflected the interests and ideas
of a given age and the objects with which that age had daily come
in contact, it was natural that every possible example of exactness
should be brought forth. But the real explanation of Wood's attitude
is found in his belief that accuracy, even to the last detail, was a sign
of poetic excellence—the same belief, in fact, which Blackwell had
expressed in his *Enquiry*. Let us examine it for a moment.

Early in his book Wood states that "that Poem must longest survive,
which abounds most in the great tragic passions, and partakes least
of the fluctuating manners of common life."[4] Because Homer "has
represented men better, than they are,"[5] because there are fewer
transient and more universal elements in the *Iliad* than in the *Odyssey*,
the former poem has always been considered superior to the latter.
To some extent, then, Wood agrees with the neoclassicists. But, whenever he speaks of Homer as an imitator of "nature," he gives an interpretation foreign to the criticism of Le Bossu, Boileau, and André
Dacier. For instance, he says that Homer's descriptions of the various
winds indicate that the poet had "an extensive Knowledge of Nature";[6] and his narrations of voyages show a great exactness "with
regard to those minute circumstances of nature and truth."[7] He even
admits that Homer may have "followed Truth and Nature, both as

---

2. Wood says, "I cannot help thinking, that those, who wish to be thoroughly acquainted, either with the manners and characters of Homer's age, of the landscape and
geography of his country, will be disappointed, if they expect to find them in this
translation." *Idem*, p. 78.

3. *Idem*, p. 85.   4. *Idem*, p. x.   5. *Idem*, p. 301.
6. *Idem*, p. 65.   7. *Idem*, p. 69.

to facts and characters, too closely" for the instruction of mankind.[8] Examples of this kind show that, instead of confining the term "nature" to idealized representations of humanity and instead of maintaining that art followed the suggestions of a creative power (nature), Wood thinks that Homer's greatest glory lay in merely transcribing what he saw, whether men or animals, mountains or plains.[9] Truth and nature practically become synonymous terms, signifying little more than a careful reproduction of facts of all kinds. Obviously, the neoclassicist would scoff at such an interpretation and would deny that "he enters most into the spirit of the Copy, who is best acquainted with the original,"[1] unless that original was merely the qualities and passions of men. Why should it be necessary to go to Greece to see how well Homer had "imitated nature," if the term implied something besides a photographic picture of landscapes and geography and the customs and manners of certain Eastern nations? Why was it impossible to test Homer's ability as a poet by one's knowledge of men in all parts of the world, irrespective of nationality?[2]

In analyzing the manners of Homer's epics, Wood did not base his observations solely upon a thorough study of the *Iliad* and *Odyssey* or merely make the bald statement that the poet had faithfully represented men as he found them in the heroic age. For he compared the Homeric characters with the less-refined Greeks of the present day and with such of their neighbors as had preserved the mode of life and the customs of antiquity.[3] The Eastern traveller, Wood says, "will discover a general resemblance between the ancient and present manners of those countries, so striking, that we cannot without injustice to our subject pass it over unnoticed."[4] He then points out that among the modern Arabians and among the Greeks of old there prevails the same oriental dissimulation: "the arts of

8. *Idem*, p. 200.

9. Wood says, "In short, it is impossible to be so much interested in the justest representations of Nature, which we never saw, as in those, which come home to our own experience of life." *Idem*, p. 172. While Homer is "the most constant and faithful copier after Nature" (*idem*, p. 5), Virgil "has deviated both from Homer, and Nature" by misrepresenting a certain group of mountains. *Idem*, p. 138. The neoclassicist might have agreed that Homer gives us a copy of universal "nature" by describing men as he saw them but he would scarcely make the term "nature" as all-inclusive as Wood does.

1. *Idem*, p. ix.

2. With qualifications, the neoclassicist would agree with Wood's following statement: "If, therefore, we would do the Poet justice, we should approach, as near as possible, to the time and place, when and where, he wrote." *Ibid*.

3. Wood observes that "American manners might also have a place here, and bear testimony to the truth of Homer's picture of human nature; but though, in some respects, savage manners have full as much dignity, as those of the Heroic, or any age . . . ; yet in general their stage of civilization is too far short of that, which the Poet describes, to come under our present consideration." *Idem*, pp. 155–6, n.

4. *Idem*, p. 144.

disguise are in those countries the great arts of life."[5] Because of the lack of a centralized government and of judges to settle all disagreements, both peoples take it into their own hands "to destroy the aggressor" who had threatened to destroy them.[6] Cruelty and injustice naturally result; and one finds "that both the antient and modern history of the East is a continued narrative of bloodshed and treachery," of homicide and brutality.[7]

It has been pointed out repeatedly that a great many critics of the time either idealized or condemned Homeric society (and hence Homeric poetry) according to whether or not they chose to emphasize the more savage or the more simple, peaceful manners of the *Iliad* and *Odyssey*. It has also been pointed out that in making an estimate of heroic times they often selected the actions of an Achilles *or* those of a Nausicaa as the criteria for judging the age as a whole. However, like Blackwell and a few Scotch writers, Wood tried to give an impartial view of the primitive Greeks. Having attributed the brutality of early societies to the absence of government, he went on to explain that, paradoxical as it might seem, the insecurity and "defective police" of the Eastern nations also led to the cultivation of hospitality. It is a "happy substitute of positive law," he says;[8] it "supplies the place of justice," erecting a bond between tribes or communities which "despise legislation" and "deny the perfect rights of mankind."[9] Similarly, Wood thinks that the absence of romantic love and the low position of women among the ancient and modern Greeks, Jews, and Arabs were detrimental to their respective societies.[1] But the lack of refinement, of polite intercourse between the sexes, somewhat compensated for this defect. Speaking of the inability of the Eastern peoples to indulge in banter and in witty or humorous conversation, he says that the "attentions of rude society are barely sufficient for the necessaries of life";[2] and that, consequently, it is not until "false appetites and imaginary wants are created," until "the various vices, follies, and affectations, of a wealthy, commercial, free people" develop, that pleasantry comes into existence. Nor can we expect to find the "artful and refined compliment" so characteristic of Virgil's poetry and that of modern times. Homer

5. *Idem*, p. 159.   6. *Idem*, p. 161.   7. *Ibid.*
8. *Idem*, p. 162.   9. *Ibid.*

1. Wood explains that there was the same indifference to women in the Greek, Arab, and Jewish societies of old. Women would have had a more prominent place in Homer's poems had it not been that "this passion, according to our ideas of it, was unknown to the manners of that age." *Idem*, p. 168. Wood adds that "The Prude and Coquette . . . are as much beyond Homer's knowledge of life, as his employing royal beauty in the meanest offices of domestic drudgery falls short of the refined attentions of modern gallantry." *Idem*, pp. 168–9.

2. *Idem*, p. 176.

was "less courtly" and "therefore more natural." A poet of a simple age, he did not belong to any sect of philosophers or to any group of politicians.[3] Thus we see that careful observation of the countries of the East and an impartial comparison of their inhabitants with the Greeks of many centuries ago led Wood to say much for and against the Homeric age. Judging by some of his remarks, it might be added that the traveller could be in certain respects a more competent critic than the scholar who read Homer's poems only in the confines of his study.

Turning from the society to the poet, what had Wood to say about Homer himself? Had he anything to contribute to a new conception of the Greek bard? In the *Enquiry*, it may be remembered, Blackwell presented the confused picture of Homer as an impecunious, strolling bard and at the same time as one of the great teachers, sages, and prophets of his age. Blackwell described how and where he might have gained his knowledge of the mysteries of the origin of the world and might have learned the secrets of the Egyptian religion—all those facts which were conveyed to his audience by means of allegorical language and incident. Wood mentions Blackwell's theory, but only in order to refute it.[4] Instead of imagining the poet listening attentively to the wise words of instructors and priests, he insists that Homer had never been to Egypt and, consequently, that his theology must have had its origin in "an accurate and comprehensive observation of Nature, under the direction of a fine imagination, and a sound understanding."[5] The religious truths to be found in the Homeric poems are only those which are obvious to any man of sense, "who looking abroad and consulting his own breast, as Homer did, compares what he sees with what he feels, and from the whole draws fair conclusions."[6] Furthermore, those portions of his mythology which fail to show the proper reverence for the gods were probably "founded in popular legends and vulgar opinion, for which every good poet, from Homer to Shakespeare, has thought proper to have great complaisance."[7]

In addition to denying the bard any understanding of formal religious doctrines, Wood refused to believe that he had any knowledge of the various arts and sciences. Thinking of such critics as Le

3. *Idem*, pp. 199–200. Like Blackwell and the primitivists, Wood draws a sharp contrast between the simple "natural" poetry of Homer and the "elegant" poetry of Virgil.

4. *Idem*, p. 117.   5. *Idem*, pp. 125–6.

6. *Idem*, p. 127. Wood remarks, "As to the conformity of style and sentiment between those Hebrew writers, and the poet, it is no more, than what we are to expect in just copies of the same original: nor does it seem at all necessary to account for the agreement from Homer's supposed knowledge of the Jewish learning through the Egyptian priests, as some ingenious men have too loosely conjectured." *Idem*, p. 156.

7. *Idem*, p. 129.

Bossu and André Dacier, he says that "Homer's deep political and ethic plan has been carried much farther than he intended,"[8] that "the Greek Poet found great part of his moral in his fable; and did not, like Virgil, invent a fable for his moral."[9] There is no doubt that Homer was a careful observer, seeing and learning much that the ordinary man in that age would have missed. But, says Wood, the poet knew no more about the science of geography than he knew about astronomy;[1] he was equally ignorant about painting and architecture;[2] and, if we had any way of ascertaining his knowledge of arithmetic, we would probably find that Homer was merely able to count upon his fingers.[3]

Though such statements may not at first seem important, it should be borne in mind that there was a growing tendency in the eighteenth century to disregard the neoclassic theory that Homer was a blazing star in a dark age, that as a great conscious artist he was unhampered by the limitations of so barbaric a period. By making him a "voice" of that age, a representative of its thoughts and feelings, Blackwell had helped to destroy this theory, even as the primitivists did after him.[4] But it was Wood's task to go still further, to deny Homer any understanding of the religious mysteries of Egypt or of any kind of knowledge which required more than a keen mind and a willingness to observe. Excepting his natural gift for such observation and an ability to express himself, how could he essentially differ from most of his contemporaries? Was it not true that the readiness with which critics refused Homer a great superiority over other men of his time was tending to make him a kind of *Volksdichter?*

Had Wood's contributions to Homeric criticism been no greater than this, we should have no great cause to consider his *Essay* in detail. But there is one chapter in the work which alone earns him a prominent place among the English critics of the century. Entitled "Homer's Language and Learning," that chapter deals with the important problem which Wolf was to dwell upon in his *Prolegomena:* namely, whether or not the Greek poet knew anything about the art of writing. Before discussing Wood's views, however, something must

8. *Idem,* p. xiii.   9. *Idem,* pp. 234–5.
1. *Idem,* p. 267.   2. *Idem,* pp. 271–2.
3. *Idem,* p. 266. Wood says that Homer's merit as a teacher lay in his having given us "a correct abstract of human nature, impartially exhibited under the circumstances, which belonged to his period of society, as far as his experience and observation went." *Idem,* p. xiii. Commenting on the criticism of men like Le Bossu, he says, "I could wish, that those, who think so highly of the mysterious wisdom of the ancients . . . would tell us, by what method they acquired it." *Idem,* p. 234.
4. Blackwell believed that the sciences had made some advance by the time of Homer. Wood, on the other hand, considered Homer's age more primitive and was therefore unwilling to grant the bard any kind of scientific knowledge.

be said about the French, English, and Scotch critics who had previously treated the subject.

It was a common theory of the eighteenth century that verse had originated long before prose, for verse was recognized as the earliest means of preserving the memory of historical events, of public transactions, and of laws among the primitive tribes of Asia and America as well as among the Greeks of the heroic age.[5] The use of meter, it was said, made it easier for the priests and bards to remember the details of the longer compositions. Convinced of these facts and knowing that Homer lived in an early period, neoclassic critics might have suspected that the Greek poet himself had never written down his verses, if it had not been for two things. In the first place, they were unable to see how such lengthy works as the *Iliad* and *Odyssey* could have been retained by memory without impairing their perfect order; and, in the second place, they felt that the language was too highly developed to have been used by one of the earliest and presumably one of the most illiterate of poets. However, when Blackwell and the Scotch primitivists began to characterize Homer as an inspired bard who sang to enraptured audiences, it no longer seemed improbable that the two epics might have been preserved for posterity by word of mouth. For example, Anselm Bayly says that in Homer's time writing was rarely practised, and that the poet's compositions were among the first works to be written down. Citing the testimony of the scholar Josephus, he thinks it even conceivable that Homer "did not write but only sung his Poems like Orpheus, Museus and other Bards of old to the People in the Streets, who learnt to repeat them by Heart."[6] John Brown apparently excluded Homer from consideration when he remarked that the "elder Poets of GREECE" always sang their verses and did not commit them to writing. But, since he admits that Homer recited his *Iliad* and *Odyssey* to audiences, it is easy to see how someone might inquire whether the Greek bard could not be included among those "elder Poets."[7] Perhaps the best expression of this view is to be found in James Beattie's essay "Of Poetry and Musick" (written in 1762).

Let it be observed too, that Homer composed his immortal work at a time when writing was not common; when people were rather hearers than readers of poetry, and could not often enjoy the pleasure even of hearing it; and when, consequently, the frequent repetition of certain words and phrases, being a help to memory, as well as to right apprehension of the

5. See the preceding chapter for some general remarks on this subject.
6. Anselm Bayly, *An Introduction to Languages, Literary and Philosophical; Especially to the English, Latin, Greek, and Hebrew: Exhibiting at One View Their Grammar, Rationale, Analogy and Idiom* (London, 1758), p. 49.
7. Brown, *Dissertation on Poetry and Music*, p. 105.

poet's meaning, would be thought rather a beauty than a blemish. The same thing is observable in some of our old ballads.[8]

Cautious as the others might be in questioning whether Homer ever used the written word, Rousseau frankly confessed that "Il m'est venu bien souvent dans l'esprit de douter nonseulement qu'Homère sût écrire, mais même qu'on écrivît de son temps."[9] Because there is no mention of writing in either poem and because so many authorities state that the *Iliad* was sung rather than read, the French critic could find no ground for supposing that the two epics were inscribed in books. Furthermore, if Homer had understood the art of writing and if his countrymen had been great readers, would not one expect to find the use of a literary language in the *Iliad* and *Odyssey* instead of such a haphazard mixture of the various Greek dialects?[1]

The theories regarding Ossian undoubtedly contributed something to this type of criticism. If the Scotch bard had recited his verses and if these verses had been handed down from father to son for nearly fifteen hundred years, it seemed conceivable that Homer's poems had been repeated by the bard himself and by the later rhapsodists until they were put in writing by a Lycurgus or a Pisistratus. If the twenty thousand verses of Ossian could be transmitted in this manner, why was it impossible that the two lengthy epics of Homer were perpetuated after the same fashion? An interesting passage on this subject occurs in Cameron's defense of the authenticity of *Fingal*.

We have already shewn that the Transactions of all Nations, before the Introduction of Letters, were couched in Verse, and handed down to Posterity by Persons who made it their sole Study to learn these Compositions themselves, and teach them to others. This was the first Origin of Poetry: hence the *Greek* 'Aoidoi or *Rhapsodists,* of whom *Homer* himself was one; hence the *Scalds* or *Scalders* of *Scandinavia;* hence the *Euhages* or *Bardi* of *Gaul;* hence the *Senachies* and *Ferdan* of the *Irish* and *Scotch.* The great Number that lived by this Profession, whose whole Time was taken up in repeating them in Public, and teaching them to others, made them not only Masters of the longest Compositions, but rendered it impossible that any worth preserving should be lost.[2]

As it was pointed out earlier, comparisons of this kind were surprisingly rare and were never direct or dealt with in great detail. But it appears likely that the excitement about the origin of the Ossianic

---

8. *The Works of James Beattie,* v. 263, n.

9. "Essai sur l'origine des langues," in *Oeuvres complètes de J. J. Rousseau,* I, 380.

1. *Ibid.* Noting that writing was unknown in the period of the Trojan War, Goguet says that, because of the polished language used by Homer, "l'écriture a dû nécessairement devenir commune entre l'espace de tems qui s'est écoulé depuis la guerre de Troye jusqu'au siécle d'Homère." Goguet, *De l'Origine des loix,* II, 236.

2. Cameron, *The Fingal of Ossian,* p. 43, Preface.

poems encouraged one or two critics, and Wood in particular, to investigate the possibility that Homer's epics were handed down orally from generation to generation.

To assemble the various theories about early writing, to discuss the invention of alphabets, and to apply the relevant facts toward forming a new theory about the origin of the *Iliad* and *Odyssey*—this was the task which Wood undertook. Agreeing with the other critics that Homer makes no mention of an art of writing in either of his poems, he stated that a system of letters was probably not used until five hundred years before Christ and that up to that time every composition was preserved by memory alone. Homer's appeal to Mnemosyne to aid him in giving the catalogue of ships, the absence of an alphabet among other primitive peoples long after they had begun to use verse, and the prominent position of the rhapsodists in all early societies were suggested as evidence that the Greek epics were not transcribed until a comparatively late period. "As to the difficulty of conceiving how Homer could acquire, retain, and communicate, all he knew, without the aid of Letters; it is, I own, very striking."[3] Nevertheless, the Mexicans repeated to the invading Spaniards lengthy poetical accounts of their history, and certain persons have collected the long compositions of the bards of Ireland, "whose accounts have been merely traditional."[4] In a day of treatises and dictionaries, Wood says, we have little conception of the powers of memory in those times "when all a man could know, was all he could remember," and when only the most vital matters were learned by rote.[5]

Although the use of verse may be found even in the savage state, writing and the use of an alphabet "must have been the result of much deep thought and reflection."[6] Had there been an art of inscription in Homer's time, we should expect to find the other arts developed to a considerable degree. But the reverse is true. Wood points out that the Greeks had such an elementary knowledge of geography, astronomy, sculpture, and architecture, and their manners were so truly those of a primitive folk that one cannot believe they were either desirous or capable of using anything so complicated as an alphabet for the preservation of words. "Without Letters, it may be said, there could be no effectual method, either of ascertaining or promulgating the sense of law; but this corresponds exactly with the wretched state of government, which we have described under the article of Manners."[7]

3. Wood, *op. cit.*, p. 259. 4. *Ibid.*
5. *Idem*, p. 260. 6. *Idem*, p. 249.
7. *Idem*, p. 263. Wood says that "the art of establishing that wonderful intercourse between the senses of hearing and seeing, by means of arbitrary marks, that have no

How, then, were the *Iliad* and *Odyssey* composed and transmitted to posterity? Early in his *Essay,* Wood says that in all probability the Greek poet was a wandering bard who chanted or recited his compositions to his countrymen, a belief "which is favoured by the dramatic cast" of his epics.[8] In this later chapter he unequivocally states that the works of Homer were sung, that he left no "written copy" of them, and consequently that one has every reason for believing that "Lycurgus brought them from Ionia into Greece, where they were known before only by scraps and detached pieces."[9] Pisistratus also may have been concerned in their preservation. "But there would have been no occasion for each of these persons to have sought so diligently for the parts of these poems, and to have arranged them so carefully," if complete "editions" had previously existed.[1] In the most interesting passage of his entire book, Wood declares:

If therefore the Spartan Lawgiver, and the other personages committed to writing, and introduced into Greece, what had been before only sung by the Rhapsodists of Ionia, just as some curious fragments of ancient poetry have been lately collected in the northern parts of this island, their reduction to order in Greece was a work of taste and judgment: and those great names which we have mentioned might claim the same merit in regard to Homer, that the ingenious Editor of Fingal is entitled to from Ossian.[2]

Here, then, was the first *direct* comparison between the manner of preserving the Scotch and the Greek poems, a comparison which, besides bringing the names of Homer and Ossian together in yet another way, was to be considered closely by many of the later English and German critics.[3]

Shocking as this theory may have seemed to some people, Wood goes on to say that Homer's illiteracy had certain salutary effects. Like the primitivists, he points out that abstract terms, which "rather impede than forward the Poet's views,"[4] are usually introduced into a highly perfected language. But Homer arrived upon the scene when language and poetry were still "entirely addressed to the ear,"[5] when simplicity and clarity were necessary if one wished to be

---

resemblance to the idea, which is by agreement affixed to them," belongs to a later period of society. *Idem,* pp. 248–9.

8. *Idem,* p. 22.   9. *Idem,* p. 278.

1. *Idem,* pp. 278–9.

2. *Idem,* p. 279. Wood says: "When the Rhapsodists recited Homer from written copies, the whole was in capitals, without punctuation, aspiration, or any marks or intervals to distinguish words. This has been the chief cause of the false readings in Homer." *Idem,* p. 289, n. The rhapsodists presumably used written copies after Lycurgus had assembled the poems.

3. For example, see Heyne's review in F. A. Wolf's *Prolegomena ad Homerum* (Halis Saxonum, 1884), p. 265, and the letters in the *Report of the Committee of the Highland Society,* Mackenzie, ed., pp. 64, 67, 75, of the Appendix.

4. Wood, *op. cit.,* p. 280.   5. *Ibid.*

understood, when every word conveyed some distinct meaning to an audience, and when, because it was always recited, poetry was more dramatic than philosophic. As a result, "we find in Homer nothing out of the reach of an ordinary capacity, and plain understanding: and those who look farther, seem to neglect his obvious beauties."[6] "Nature," Wood concludes, is the one concern of a genius like Homer; and a language associated with "imperfect arts, simple manners, and unlettered society, best suits his purpose."[7]

Wood made at least two important contributions to Homeric criticism. In the first place, he challenged the only remaining unchallenged theory associated with neoclassicism, one which, while it may have been overlooked, had not been rejected even by primitivists and progressivists. According to that theory, Homer had been the source of all knowledge in his day. He had been both sage and prophet, the teacher of an ignorant people—as some said, a blazing star in a dark age. Wood discarded this view entirely because, as he said, it was merely traditional. There was nothing, no evidence internal or external, to prove that Homer had understood the intricacies of astronomy, mathematics, and religion—all that was to be known in his day. In fact, one may question whether he was more learned than most of his contemporaries, whether his references to the sciences were more profound than those which the average person could have made. Trifling as the point may seem, it did make it easier than ever to regard Homer as the simple, impassioned bard, as the ignorant singer transmitting the traditions of his people. He was one of them, not superior to them, a primitive Greek, not an erudite man of the world.

Perhaps growing out of this theory was Wood's belief that Homer could not write. One might expect that it would have made some stir among English critics, at least among those who considered Homer a primitive bard and who, for a long time, had been talking about the origins of poetry. Strangely enough, only a handful of critics even mentioned Wood's idea.[8] The others either had not read the *Essay*, English editions being scarce, or they did not fully realize the implications of such a theory. In fact, Wood himself may not have been

---

6. *Idem*, p. 286. 7. *Idem*, p. 280.

8. As it was pointed out earlier, the only hostile review of the *Essay* appeared in *Critical Observations on Books, Antient and Modern*, in 1776. Wood was often cited in Mitford's *History of Greece*, but Mitford made no attempt to elaborate upon Wood's theories. An interesting passage occurs in Kames, *Sketches of the History of Man*, I, 173–4: "There is no appearance that writing was known in Greece so early as the time of Homer; for in none of his works is there any mention of it. This, it is true, is but negative evidence; but negative evidence must always command our assent, where no positive evidence stands in opposition. If it was known, it must have been newly introduced; and used probably to record laws, religious precepts, or other short compositions."

aware how radically it could, and later would, affect the general conception of Homer. If Homer had not known how to write, there is less reason than ever to distinguish him from his contemporaries. He must have been as superstitious and ignorant as they, as firm a believer in the fantastic tales of heroes and gods. More important yet, he could hardly have been a composer of long and orderly epics. A poet who cannot write must be regarded as a kind of balladist, telling traditional stories and episodes which poets after him were to tell again and again with inevitable alterations.

It was Wolf and the Continental critics who saw these implications and shocked the world with their theories about Homer. In fact, since several of the later commentators were influenced by the studies of Wood and his predecessor, Blackwell, it may be worth while to consider for a moment the importance of both the *Enquiry* and the *Essay* in France and Germany.

Herder was perhaps the first to call attention to the *Enquiry* and the first to espouse the arguments of the professor of Greek. In his essays "Ueber die neuere deutsche Litteratur" (1767), he declares that critics should make every attempt to understand the relationship of the poet to his age, that, whether translating him or criticizing him, they should view the bard "wie er ist."[9] "Ein Erklärer der Griechen soll ihren Geist der Nation, der Zeit, des Landes und der Lebensart kennen."[1] Unfortunately, the Germans had not realized the value of such knowledge or the merit of the historical approach in general. "Wie sehr haben uns die Engländer hier schon vorgearbeitet?" Herder asks. He immediately answers the question by pointing to Blackwell's *Enquiry* as "dies schäzzbare Buch," which "zum Homer ein Schlüssel ist," an introduction to the real nature of the Greek poems.[2] Though he was undoubtedly well acquainted with the writings of the primitivists, the treatises on original genius, and the historical studies of Thomas and Joseph Warton and Richard Hurd, Herder's remarks on Homer throughout these essays bear a striking resemblance to the opinions of Blackwell.[3] For example, he says that "in

9. *Herders sämmtliche Werke*, Bernhard Suphan, ed. (Berlin, 1877–1913), I, 289.
1. *Idem*, II, 144.
2. *Idem*, I, 289. Herder remarks, "Denn nie hätten die Perraults in Frankreich und Deutschland über das Lächerliche Göttliche und Hässliche in Homer so feine Bemerkungen, Programm's und Briefe geschrieben, wenn sie sich mit dem Dichter in eine Zeit, Nation, und Stellung hätten setzen können." *Idem*, II, 161.
3. In a review of Denis' translation of Ossian's poems, Herder speaks of some of the English critics. "Die Engländer haben also auch auf diesem Wege fast die schönsten Sachen zur Kritik erhalten. Warton über Pope und Spenser, Addison über Milton, Hurd über Horaz, Blackwell über Homer, so viele Gute und Böse über Shakespear, hier zwei edle Leute, (zu denen sich noch in den Noten Cesarotti gesellet) über Ossian—und was haben wir Deutschen nun dagegen?" Suphan, *op. cit.*, v, 330. An examination of Suphan's index shows that Herder frequently cited passages in Blackwell's *Enquiry*.

seinem Lande, in den Zeitläuften vor und neben ihm, kurz bei der Natur bleibt er und schildert sie mit Würde";[4] and he agrees that "die Jugend der Poesie ist, wie die Jugend der Menschlichen Natur, würksam und ihre Kräfte bewegend."[5] Again, he states that "bei Homer ist noch alles Natur . . . Der Gesang is rauh und prächtig: die Sitten roh und auf dem Gipfel Menschlicher Stärke: die Götter niedrig und erhaben: . . . alles ein Zeuge der Natur, die durch ihn sang."[6] The insistence upon the need for historical interpretation, the belief that in copying nature Homer had succeeded as he could not have succeeded in a later age, and the conception of the Greek poet as a voice of his time had all been developed by Blackwell and were the focal points both in the *Enquiry* and in Herder's Homeric criticism.

In France an important translator of the *Iliad* paid tribute to Blackwell by using material from his book for a long introductory essay upon the Greek poet. Remarking that "plusieurs causes physiques & morales contribuent à former les grands hommes,"[7] Rochefort reviews the effects of climate, manners, and religion upon Homer's compositions, shows how society had advanced beyond barbarity at the same time that it had not reached a state of refinement, and observes that the poet could behold the downfall of cities, on the one hand, and the beginnings of art and settled government, on the other.[8] Like Herder and, for that matter, like most of Blackwell's admirers, this critic emphasized the need for viewing Homer as he really was, as an inspired bard of a primitive time; and he called attention to the poet's imagination, his simplicity, and his love for the fabulous. He censures Pope for having abandoned "ce beau naturel, cette simplicité sobre & facile, cette rapidité & cette perfection d'idées, qui ravissent dans la lecture d'Homere."[9] Again, as a follower of Blackwell, he shows a hostile attitude toward the neoclassicists: "Qu'importe la Poëtique d'Aristote à qui peut lire Homere? L'unité, la simplicité d'action, voilà la premiere régle du Poëme épique. Qui la prescrivit à Homere? son génie & la nécessité."[1]

Taking into consideration the fact that Blackwell's book had been

---

4. "Ueber die neuere deutsche Litteratur," in Suphan, *op. cit.*, II, 168.
5. *Idem*, II, 151.
6. *Idem*, I, 174, n. Like Blackwell, Herder remarks, "Wenn ich den Homer lese, so stehe ich im Geist in Griechenland auf einem versammleten Markte, und stelle mir vor, wie der Sänger Io im Plato die Rhapsodien seines göttlichen Dichters mir vorsinget." *Idem*, I, 176.
7. M. de Rochefort, *L'Iliade d'Homere, traduite en vers, avec des remarques & un discours sur Homere* (Paris, 1772), I, 3.
8. *Idem*, I, 1–15. Rochefort mentions the *Enquiry* in one of his footnotes. (*Idem*, I, 15.)
9. *Idem*, I, 52.   1. *Idem*, I, 76.

cited by such writers as Thomas and Joseph Warton, Elizabeth Montagu, Richard Hurd, Edward Young, Hugh Blair, James Beattie, and Robert Wood, that it was admired by so important a writer as Herder, that it was also known to Heyne[2] and Wolf,[3] and that it was translated into German by J. H. Voss in 1776,[4] we can say, I think, that the *Enquiry* played a rather conspicuous part in the development of the historical approach, first in England and later on the Continent. Writers may not always have accepted its arguments but many used its method in their criticism of literature.

Possibly because Blackwell had based the larger part of his book on conjectures and assumptions which could not be proved or disproved, the French and German critics of the latter part of the century usually turned to Wood's *Essay* for suggestions. Six years before the English public knew about the work (in 1769), its author sent a copy to J. D. Michaelis,[5] who showed it to Heyne, who in turn reviewed it in one of the Göttingen magazines. "Die *Enquiry into the Life and Writings of Homer* liegt zwar gewissermassen zum Grunde," Heyne boldly announces; for a work has just appeared which has entirely superseded the earlier one by Blackwell, a work written by a man "welcher auf der Stelle gewesen ist, wo Homer sang, Achill focht und Ulyss reisste." "Noch niemanden haben wir gesehen, der so tief in den Geist Homers eingedrungen wäre."[6] Following this brief introduction, Heyne points out the necessity of realizing that the Greek poet lived in another climate, in an early period of society when men were just beginning to emerge "aus dem ersten rohen Zustand der Natur" and had made few advances in the arts and sciences.[7] Only through travel books and the accounts of the uncivilized inhabitants of other lands can one approach the age of Homer[8]—only through books such as the one written by Wood. "Mit diesem Himmel von Ionien, mit der Natur auf der Küste, wo unser griechische Barde der Sänger der reinen, der unverstellten Natur ward, kann Herr W. ge-

2. See below for remarks on Heyne.

3. In a letter to Heyne, dated January 9, 1796, Wolf speaks of *"Blackwell's* und *Wood's* bessere Begriffe vom Homer." The letter may be found in Wolf, *op. cit.*, p. 286.

4. It is significant that only two editions of the *Enquiry* were published in England, in 1735 and 1736, and that the Germans did not translate Blackwell's book until forty years later when they were beginning to adopt the historical approach in criticizing Homer.

5. In a letter to Michaelis, dated November 16, 1769, John Pringle says that Wood sends "his best respects" and begs "acceptance of a piece of his (here with sent), which, though printed, is not published, nor indeed finished. . . . It is an *Essay on Homer.*" Buhle, *op. cit.*, II, 238.

6. C. F. Michaelis, "Vorrede," in *Robert Woods Versuch über das Originalgenie des Homers aus dem Englischen* (Frankfort-am-Main, 1773), pp. 6–7. Heyne's review was printed as a part of the introduction.

7. *Idem*, p. 8.   8. *Idem*, pp. 8–9.

nauer, als jemand, bekannt seyn, da er in eben dieser Absicht jene Gegenden durchgereiset hat."[9]

Heyne's favorable review soon brought demands from all quarters that Wood's *Essay* be translated in Germany. "Zu Kaufe war das Buch gar nicht zu bekommen. England selbst kannte es kaum dem Namen nach, und Deutschland blos aus der Recension in den göttingischen Zeitungen."[1] At length Michaelis' son, Christian Friedrich, published a translation in 1773 and Wood's name was immediately upon the tongues of many of the important classical scholars. With great enthusiasm Goethe agreed with Heyne that one could not become an authoritative critic of Homer without seeing the land in which the poet lived and wrote and without viewing the scenes of the *Iliad* and *Odyssey*.[2] Wood had done this. "Mit den scharfsichtigsten Blicken dringt er durch die Nebel eines so fernen Abstandes bis zur eigentlichen Kultur des Homerischen Zeitalters hindurch und lehrt es uns aus dem philosophischen Standpunkte der Geschichte der Menschheit betrachten."[3] To Bryant he gives credit for having preserved "die schätzbarsten Fragmente" of a long work which Wood would probably have written if he had not died so unexpectedly,[4] and to Heyne he gives praise for having roused German scholars to attempt translations of the *Essay*.[5] How important Goethe considered works like Wood's may be gathered from the following passage in *Dichtung und Wahrheit*.

Auch das Homerische Licht ging uns neu wieder auf, und zwar recht im Sinne der Zeit, die ein solches Erscheinen höchst begünstigte: denn das beständige Hinweisen auf Natur bewirkte zuletzt, dass man auch die Werke der Alten von dieser Seite betrachten lernte. Was mehrere Reisende zu Aufklärung der heiligen Schriften getan, leisteten andere für den Homer. Durch Guys ward man eingeleitet, Wood gab der Sache den

9. *Idem*, p. 9. Speaking of Wood's *Essay*, one critic says: "Wunderbar fühlte sich Heyne davon ergriffen; manches was ihm vorher nur geahndet hatte, ward ihm jetzt plötzlich klar. Aber auch eine neue Welt von Forschungen eröffnete sich ihm zugleich! Es bedurfte nur eines solchen Beyspiels, um ihn zu lehren, was es heisse und was dazu gehöre, einen alten Dichter in dem Geist seiner Zeit und seines Volks zu lesen!" A. H. L. Heeren, *Christian Gottlob Heyne, Biographisch dargestellt* (Göttingen, 1813), p. 121.

1. Michaelis, *op. cit.*, p. 4.

2. It is perhaps worth noting that the German translation appeared two years before the large English edition. Bearing in mind the fact that a translated edition of Blackwell's *Enquiry* was published in 1776, could this mean that the Germans were becoming more interested than the English in historical interpretations of Homer?

3. *Goethes sämtliche Werke*, Eduard von der Hellen, ed. (Jubiläums-Ausgabe, Stuttgart, und Berlin, 1902–07), XXXVI, 16. These observations were made in a review of Michaelis' translation of Wood's *Essay* (1773).

4. *Ibid.*

5. *Idem*, XXXVI, 17. Before the end of the century, the *Essay* was translated into French, German, Spanish, and Italian.

Schwung. Eine Göttinger Rezension des anfangs sehr seltenen Originals machte uns mit der Absicht bekannt und belehrte uns, wie weit sie ausgeführt worden. Wir sahen nun nicht mehr in jenen Gedichten ein angespanntes und aufgedunsenes Heldenwesen, sondern die abgespiegelte Wahrheit einer uralten Gegenwart, und suchten uns dieselbe möglichst heranzuziehen.[6]

Herder was also acquainted with the *Essay*. Speaking of the book, he says that it is highly desirable to read ancient poems in the countries where they originated: "da lassen sich Skalden und Barden anders lesen, als neben dem Katheder des Professors."[7] Using the same arguments that Wood had employed, he points out that Homer lived in an early period in Ionia, that he sang the tale of Troy "auf eben so natürliche, seinem Zeitalter angenehmste, mildeste Weise," and that his poems "blieben in Ohr und Munde" of the people, until they were finally written down in the age of Lycurgus.[8] Possibly bearing in mind Wood's remarks on the transmission of the ancient Scotch and Greek poems, Herder said that "Homers Rhapsodien und Ossians Lieder waren gleichsam *impromptus*, weil man damals noch von Nichts als *impromptus* der Rede wusste";[9] and that *Temora* was the *Odyssey*, and *Fingal* the *Iliad* of the Scotch Highlanders.[1] Of all the works on ancient poetry, Herder said in 1778, "Ich will besonders und vor allen nur Blackwells Untersuchung über Homers Leben und Schriften . . . , Woods Versuch über das Originalgenie Homers . . . , Blairs Abhandlung über Ossian . . . nennen."[2]

Shortly after the *Prolegomena* appeared, an interesting episode took place in Germany, one which directly concerned Wood's *Essay*.[3] Heyne apparently wrote to Wolf, saying that the latter had used some of his theories about the origin of the art of writing. With indignation Wolf wrote back on January 9, 1796, pointing out that in

6. *Idem*, XXIV, 109–10. A few years later, Werther was passionately reading Homer and Ossian. On one occasion a young man came to Werther and, hearing that he was so deeply interested in Greek literature, "kramte viel Wissens aus, von *Batteux* bis zu *Wood*, von *de Piles* zu *Winckelmann*." *Idem*, XVI, 9.
7. "Von Deutscher Art und Kunst," in Suphan, *op. cit.*, V, 169.
8. "Ursachen des gesunknen Geschmacks bei den verschiednen Völkern, da er geblühet," in Suphan, *op. cit.*, V, 614.
9. "Von Deutscher Art und Kunst," in Suphan, *op. cit.*, V, 182.
1. Suphan, *op. cit.*, V, 329. This remark appeared in a review of Denis's translation of Ossian.
2. "Ueber die Würkung der Dichtkunst auf die Sitten der Völker in alten und neuen Zeiten," in Suphan, *op. cit.*, VIII, 341, n.
3. In France Wood's *Essay* was first translated in 1777. Even before that date, the Comte de Choiseul-Gouffier went to the East to carry on the Englishman's investigations. In his *Voyage pittoresque de la Grèce*, I (1782), Choiseul also compared Homeric descriptions with the actual appearance of the country but added little to what Wood had said. His real contributions were almost entirely of an antiquarian nature—archeological discoveries in the region of Troy.

his various reviews and longer publications Heyne had merely re-peated the well-known statements which Wood had made several years before and had added nothing of his own. Wolf had also read the *Essay*, had agreed with the English critic, and had developed new opinions about Homer's knowledge of writing from the theories laid down by Wood. At one point in this letter he says: "Ia, hätte *Wood* länger gelebt, und hätte er die ganze Materie, in die er einen der geistreichsten Blicke that, von allen Seiten als Alterthumsforscher und Kritiker beleuchten können; sicher wäre für uns beide hier wenig zu thun."[4]

Needless to say, the belief that Homer had not known how to write was of primary importance to Wolf's hypotheses and it would not be going too far to say that the argument of the *Prolegomena* hinged upon this question which Wood had raised. As posed by the English critic and as developed by Wolf, the theory gave a reasonable ex-planation why there were parts of the Homeric poems which did not seem directly concerned with the main action, why some passages did not appear to belong where they were. It explained why, supposing the two poems artistic, such carefully planned works should emerge from a barbaric society, why the language was so highly developed, and why there were mixtures of dialects and different forms for the same words. Finally, it explained the persistent reports of early writers that Lycurgus and Pisistratus had collected the parts of the *Iliad* and *Odyssey* and the failure of antiquity to agree about the facts of Homer's life.

One must not, therefore, underrate the importance of Robert Wood's work. Aside from revealing the development of a more scien-tific type of Homeric criticism, his *Essay* forms a link between the English and German writers, between those who began to use the historical approach and those who developed it further, between those who provided most of the materials and those who clearly stated a new theory of the utmost significance to the more recent criticism of Homer.

4. Wolf, *op. cit.*, pp. 276–7. Speaking of the theory that Homer did not know how to write, Wolf says: "Wenige Iahre nachher, als ich Sie *Blackwell's* und *Wood's* bessere Begriffe vom Homer in Umlauf bringen hörte, hatten Sie zwar nicht übel Lust, die Hypothese für sehr wahrscheinlich auszugeben, jedoch ohne den mindesten Grund beizufügen, den ich nicht schon bei *Wood* gelesen hatte." *Idem*, pp. 286–7.

Conclusion

IN England the historical movement naturally centered around
native poets like Chaucer, Shakespeare, and Spenser, the Elizabethan dramatists and the balladists. Some were being reëvalu-
ated, while others were being discovered and evaluated for the first
time.Textual studies and more-or-less superficial surveys of English
literature were frequently appearing. On the other hand, abundant
criticism of the British poets did not mean that the poets from the
south and east of Europe were playing unimportant rôles in this new
movement. Homer, for example, was a major figure in the Battle of Ancients and Moderns. Later he was regarded by the Scotch as one of the
two great primitive poets, inferior only to Ossian. There were also inevitable comparisons between Homer and poets other than Ossian,
some British, some not—comparisons which were rarely adequate,
often odd, but hardly to be overlooked. Then, too, theories about
Homer should be considered in any study of the relation between the
historical and neoclassical approaches. In the reëstimate of this Greek
poet, in brief, one views from a different angle the methods, prejudices, interests, and assumptions of the eighteenth-century critics
whose interpretations were mainly historical.

Perhaps the principal reason why attention should be paid to
criticism of Homer is the fact that it did not develop in the same ways
or at the same moments as criticism of the British poets. For instance,
distinctions between Homeric and modern poetry (usually French)
were being emphasized at a time when Chaucer and Spenser were
generally being ignored or at least regarded as second-rate. There is
nothing remarkable about this fact. While Homer had often been
treated as a contemporary, critics had always assumed that he was a
poet of long ago and hence believed that his country and age were
among the things they ought to consider. But a historical approach
was more often suggested than used and it was only at the end of
the seventeenth century, when there was real consciousness of the
changes wrought by time, of development and progress, that Homer's
place in history was fairly well understood. Especially to one group,
the Moderns, every poem began to seem individual. The *Iliad* was not
at all like recent epics because it belonged to the distant past. In
lacking ideas that were either Christian or "rational," it was simply
out-of-date and valueless to the present-day reader. For a time the
Ancients stuck tenaciously to the universal qualities of poetry, continuing to think of all literature as basically static and subject to

change from age to age only in its setting. When they spoke in terms of history, they of course renounced the theory of progress, in literature at least. But, the more critics argued and emphasized the "particulars" in works of art, the more it seemed the Moderns were right: the "particulars" were so obvious and so numerous that they appeared to be responsible for the essential character of a literary work, while the universal qualities were at best elusive and hard to identify. As a result, the part of the Battle revolving about Homer soon became a "battle of particulars": the customs, manners, and ways of life described by Homer. They were interpreted either as unpleasantly barbarous and shocking or as pleasantly simple and naïve—according to the way each critic had decided to consider them.

There was obviously no historical criticism in this long and bitter quarrel. Since unprejudiced attempts merely to understand and explain the relation of the poem to its backgrounds were almost nonexistent, one could hardly expect that critics would have adopted the view that literature is good only insofar as it "expresses" a particular age. Instead, they possessed merely a well-developed historical sense or perspective, an awareness that external circumstances have an effect upon works of art. Dogmatically they proclaimed that the effect was slight or that it was great and, if great, they seem to have taken it for granted that one's estimate of a poem had to depend upon his estimate of the conditioning circumstances. But there is no reason to overlook the early use of the historical approach, however remote it may seem from historical criticism. If one did so, he would be ignoring the fact that many literary theories, including those of the historical critic, eventually emerged from this awareness that history and literature have definite connections. Also, he would be disregarding the many difficulties holding up the advance of the new movement, especially the part concerning non-British poets like Homer. For example, historical interpretations were long sandwiched in among more favored and time-proven interpretations, particularly the neoclassical one. This meant that the historical approach, while not necessarily opposed to the formal approach, was to be used in a superficial way as long as the critic's first concern was universal poetic values. Also, the historical view, to be worth while, demands specialized and abundant knowledge not usually expected of the formalist—a knowledge of nonliterary as well as literary backgrounds. It demands study of all kinds of documents and records, biographical and historical, materials which earlier critics did not know how to use and which, all too often, were not even available to them. While one might unearth a good deal about the Elizabethan era and the life of Spenser, he could find practically nothing to aid him in studying Homer and many other Continental poets. The history of the Homeric age was a closed book, except for hints to be gleaned here and there in Homer himself. The facts of Homer's life were uncertain, if they were facts at all. The Greek language was often a barrier. And there was no other poetry of the Homeric period with which to compare the *Iliad*. In short, a thoroughgoing historical study of literature was to be rare until the day of the specialist dawned. It was to be the final step after readers, critics, and writers in general came, more and more, to accept and use a historical approach as perhaps the fundamental approach to every literary work. By 1700 a comparative handful of critics, largely in France, were using it. Since their sole purpose was to establish the superiority of the modern or of the ancient world, they turned to Homer only because he was the best available measure of antiquity.

During the next two decades, historical treatment of the British poets made only modest progress. It certainly did not develop at the pace which one might expect. In the case of Homer, however, despite considerable resentment of his high prestige, historical perspective was surprisingly abundant and sometimes even verged upon real historical study. Many critics were trying hard to understand Homeric backgrounds. Certainly Pope's remark concerning Homer, that "no man can tolerably understand this author" without knowing *all* the circumstances under which he wrote, gives the new approach a new significance. It shows, for one thing, that even the staunchest believer in the permanent values of art recognized the need for delving into environment. Nor was "explaining" Homer any longer confined to stereotype comments on fable, plot, and machinery. As in the notes and introductions of Mme. Dacier and Pope, it now began to mean the clarification of lines, phrases, and single words obscure to the reader because of his distance from Homeric civilization and ways of thinking. Early Greek documents and Roman commentaries were culled for further historical information on mythology, language, and customs. Since there was a suspicion that the poet's experiences might have had some bearing on his poetry, the life of Homer also was examined anew. It was no longer passed over as it had been by previous neoclassicists and even by the Moderns, or treated in the undiscriminating fashion of the encyclopedists and "biographers" of the 1600's. As a result of biographical interest, questions about the identity of Homer were raised, though no one had the slightest idea to what those questions could and would lead. Finally Mme. Dacier, Pope, Addison, and others compared Homer's poems with early poems from various parts of the world, finding likenesses they casually laid to climatic, linguistic, and social environments. Romances and ballads, and especially the Bible, had something in common with Homer's epics.

By 1735, the year of Blackwell's *Enquiry*, specific historical problems concerning Homer were still unsolved. Though literary men had been fully aware that the problems existed, most of them had talked in generalities about Homer's relation to his age or had argued interminably whether Homeric manners should be interpreted favorably or not. It was time, therefore, for a comprehensive historical study of Homer, a work which would seek to analyze everything that might possibly have influenced his poems. The *Enquiry* proved to be such a work and it did so largely because it was written by an expert on Greek literature. Blackwell, unlike earlier critics, was not forced merely to acknowledge the importance of backgrounds and then dismiss the matter for want of information. As a professor of Greek, he knew the various Greek dialects. He had command of literary and historical sources sometimes found among pedants and scholars at that time but rarely among critics. He handled his subject consistently from a single point of view, the historical, thereby avoiding the superficialities and confusion of those who had used several approaches. Years later, when sudden impetus was given to the historical movement, Blackwell's book continued to be read and cited by English critics. It was yet the outstanding critical work of the century on Homer but, more important, it demonstrated that the value of the historical approach lay in precise and scholarly study of all kinds of literary backgrounds and not merely in reminders that a given work belonged to a bygone age. It proved that the new criticism, in its complexity, demanded intensive work in language, literary indebtedness, social, political, and religious influences, to say nothing of biography. Whatever the defects of the *Enquiry* from some critics' points of view—such as its immediate assumption that Homer was the greatest poet of all time—it pointed the way for later studies of literature. One suspects, in fact, that Blackwell gave more encouragement to historical treatment of English literature than has sometimes been recognized.

Wood was Blackwell's successor—less scholarly perhaps but with the same tendencies of the specialist. For example, he was not content to view Homeric society through the *Iliad* alone or merely to compare it with Scotch society as described by Ossian. Instead, he observed closely how primitive folk of North Africa lived—what customs, daily habits, and systems of morality they had. He then tried to determine to what extent Homeric manners were typical of manners among all early peoples and to what extent they were unique. This was something like laboratory study, something like the method of the present-day anthropologist. Also, before attempting to write about the amazing exactness of Homer's descriptions, he had made detailed first-hand observations in Asia Minor and Greece, concentrating upon archeology and geography. The larger part of the *Essay*, as a result, contains a series of parallels between the ancient world as it was and as pictured by Homer, dull matter to the modern reader but significant as one of the early efforts to locate the sources of the poet's descriptive passages. While some critics were searching for Spenser's indebtedness to classical and early English literature, Wood was studying the effect of natural surroundings upon Homer's work.

Scholarly studies such as Wood's were rare indeed in England, perhaps because of the difficulties mentioned earlier, perhaps because classicists confined their work to trifling corrections of text and controversy over mythology. Not until Heyne and Wolf does interpreting and explaining of Homer appear to have been accepted as an important task of the scholar. But no figure stands out more clearly than Homer in the literary criticism of the times. He was as familiar as ever to English readers. That mass of poets, critics, historians, letter writers, and even churchmen, while amateurs in matters Greek, all had something to say about Homer, something original for the eighteenth century if not for the present day. As the real importance of history gradually dawned, it became clear that there was to be no division of labor between advocates of the two approaches, the neoclassical and the historical. As if self-sufficient, each group sought to take the center of the stage, to concern itself with the very basis of poetry. For the formalist it was the timeless qualities which made the *Iliad* "Homeric": historical setting was relatively unimportant. For the historically minded critic, environment was all that mattered, that welter of ideas and customs peculiar to Homer: timeless qualities were elusive at best and perhaps nonexistent. The true value of the *Iliad* was found, therefore, in its universal representations of human nature or in its specific pictures of Greek life— not in both. The historical approach being in the ascendancy, Homer, the rational sage, the genius who had known intuitively what was best and noblest in man, was suffered to die his slow death, while a new Homer, almost a counterpart to the old, was gradually created. He became important as the historian of a people and its wars, its traditions, its primitive religion, its strange customs and ideas. This people had existed at a certain moment in time, and so had Homer, at almost the same time. He must therefore have been like them—as impassioned, as full of imaginings, as much a lover of impossible tales and of brutal warfare and family life. Perhaps, too, he was as ignorant as they.

Two things should be made clear about the use of the new approach. In the first place, with regard to Spenser and Chaucer, historical analysis was motivated in part by the growth of nationalism, by a feeling of pride in English authors. It became customary to insist that the times had been responsible for the kind of poetry which Spenser had written and that one should refrain from testing the *Faerie Queene* by absolute criteria. Criticism of Spenser or of almost any English poet should be relative. But few critics thought that Homer should be treated in the same manner. While Blackwell, Wood, and others maintained that a particular environment had made the *Iliad* and *Odyssey* the greatest poems ever written, most critics turned to the historical approach for the sole purpose of destroying Homer, for showing how out-of-date and barbaric his ideas were. Thus it would seem that use of history was making possible a relativist view of literature on some occasions and a purely subjective view on others. It permitted one to excuse and to like the "content" of Chaucer's poems and hence Chaucer; one could find reason to excuse but rarely to like Homer's "content" or Homer.

In the second place, whatever view of Homer one might take, the historical approach was slowly forming the nineteenth-century attitude toward him and toward the epic. One can easily enough see how sympathetic studies such as Blackwell's *Enquiry* and Wood's *Essay* might substantially contribute to this attitude. Both works were translated and reviewed abroad and their conceptions of the epic poet as an inspired rhapsodist who probably could not write were widely discussed in France and Germany. But even unsympathetic criticism was important—comments to the effect that the *Iliad* was a child's fairy tale and a wild ballad about wild men. It was but a matter of time before intended destructive criticism was to be reevaluated and made constructive, before violence and romantic legends, so strenuously objected to by eighteenth-century writers, were to seem the proper matter of epic poetry. Brutes like Achilles were to be heroes again, and gods like Jove, dethroned for a hundred years, were to be restored. Even if one might refuse to idolize Homer, he would at least insist upon relative standards in criticizing him, upon understanding him in connection with his environment. New literary theories were to arise and, remarkably enough, almost every eighteenth-century critic who used a historical approach, whatever his particular purpose, was helping to develop these theories.

It would be hard to say whether patriotic reëstimation of Shakespeare or the mingled idealization of and opposition to Homer in England had the greater effect upon later criticism. Such a matter cannot be determined, nor need it be. But if doubt remains as to the importance of English Homeric criticism, to later epic theory at least, Scotch criticism leaves little room for dispute. As we have seen, the Scotch were intent upon winning respect for Ossian and, to do so, were trying to find reasons why he should share Homer's long-established reputation as an epic poet. They turned, naturally enough, to historical analysis rather than neoclassic criteria. If one limited oneself to customs and manners, to supernatural elements, and to ways of life—above all, if he did not consider them in too much detail—it was possible to prove that Ossian and Homer were amazingly alike. Similar backgrounds had produced similar poets. Even when differences were touched upon, as often they were, it was easy to imagine that they were not important enough to warrant careful discussion. Hence Homer and Ossian seemed about on a level.

If efforts were made to bring Ossian up to Homer's level, attempts to sink Homer below Ossian's were far more abundant. For this purpose the differences were emphasized, while the similarities were not. In fact, critics were busily demonstrating that the backgrounds of the two poets were almost incomparable, that the climate, religion, and ways of life of Greeks and Highlanders were as different as day and night. Even if Ossian and Homer were outstanding examples of early poets, there were good reasons—"historical" reasons—why the former should seem the ideal bard, spontaneous and yet refined, and the latter should appear far too primitive even for a primitivist. The stories Homer told were necessarily fantastic, his gods childish compared to Ossian's respectable ghosts, and his heroes, ferocious beings, lacking in that almost modern sentimentality which characterized Ossian's. Homer's heroes, because Greek, were cruel and contemptuous toward women, selfish and erratic, given to excess in eating and drinking. Homer would stop at nothing, however repugnant; Ossian seemed mild and polite by comparison. If Ossian had too little restraint, Homer had none.

What ordinarily distinguishes the Scotch writers from the English is, of course, their preference for early, emotional poetry. To be sure, Homer was still an ideal bard for men like Duff and Ferguson, though at times even they had some qualms about the violence and lack of sensibility on the part of his characters. He was a spontaneous, blind (and, to Beattie, unlettered) singer with a fertile imagination, a rhapsodist whose domestic scenes and accounts of filial loyalty were to be relished by discriminating readers. But in general the Scotch showed more hostility and prejudice than understanding and kindliness toward Homer, arguing against him in a manner that is not easily explained. For instance, it is odd that those who thought so highly of spontaneity should find too much of it in any poet, particularly in Homer, and that they did not instead object to Homer because of his refinement and polish, qualities supposedly distasteful to the primitivist. They might have added that painstaking attention to form had rendered impossible any free play of imagination, that the *Iliad*, unlike *Fingal*, was too consciously planned to be a good poem. There may be reasons why the Scotch did not argue in this fashion—such as their rejection of all neoclassic opinions, of Homer or anyone else, and their tendency to estimate all poetry on the basis of content. The fact nevertheless remains that, while they acknowledged Homer to be as much an original genius as Ossian, they formed, with Blackwell's help, some fairly definite ideas about what was properly primitive and what was not. As might be expected, fidelity to Ossian was largely responsible for their distinction between the primitive and the barbaric, and hence for their conception of the true early epic. An epic poet had to be like Ossian to be great and of course there could be no one like him.

In all this criticism of Homer and Ossian, one thing seems particularly evident. Neoclassicism, with its long-established standards and rules, had obliged the critic to approach every poem in much the same way and even to arrive at conclusions which were not substantially different from other critics'. This was not the case with the historical approach, for there were no time-tested rules, no beaten tracks to follow. All that the use of history obliged one to do was to consider the poet in relation to his environment. He could then set up his own rules, or modify the arbitrary rules of others, or, if intent only on explaining, have no rules at all. For example, the common view that Homer's poems were primarily valuable as historical documents was not the inevitable result of using the historical approach. Nor was one forced to think of Homer as a mere political historian, relating events of a little-known epoch of Greece's past. There were many possible ways in which this approach could be applied and it was up to the individual critic at the start whether he wished to use history in evaluating literature or literature in reconstructing the past.

It is not strange, then, that Scotch criticism of Homer, or, for that matter, Homeric criticism in general, often seems rather bewildering when one looks back at the eighteenth century. It took all forms. Even when critics preferred to use history in making literary appraisals, in judging Homer's merit as a poet, there seems to have been no agreement at all. Individual standards meant that Ossian would reign supreme for some critics, that Ossian and Homer were both great primitive poets for others, and for another group that Chaucer, or Spenser, or Tasso—or Homer—should be regarded as the greatest of all. Nor was it always that the poet's content was more pleasing, more vivid, more instructive, or more "poetic," since critics sometimes preferred a poet like Ossian because he was more readily understood or simply because he was Scotch. In the latter case, an opinion of the poet apparently determined one's opinion of the poem!

The nineteenth century of course inherited all these uses of the historical approach and it too had its bitter quarrels about Homer.

But the quarrels involved scholars for the most part, men whose primary concern was whether a Homer had or had not existed rather than how his poetry should be interpreted. Among literary critics there was less disagreement than heretofore. There was certainly less tendency to regard Homer in eighteenth-century fashion as the best or worst poet because his environment had been the best or worst that the critic could imagine—that is, utterly barbaric or ideally primitive. While thoroughgoing relative criticism was a late development, many critics around 1800 began to think that a poem should be viewed as an expression of a particular society. Take, for example, Mme. de Staël's *De l'Allemagne.* Instead of estimating the virtues and vices of Greeks, Germans, or Frenchmen, and hence of their literatures, she turns to history to show that there have been two great eras in the past, the classical and the romantic, and as a result two distinct kinds of literature. The epic belongs to the classical period. In a statement reminding one faintly of Blackwell, she says that the *Iliad* required "un concours singuler de circonstances qui s'est recontré que chez les Grecs"—above all, a particular kind of language and the sort of "imagination" possible only in the heroic age. German literature, on the other hand, is called romantic and, more specifically, lyrical—a fact which is to be explained in terms of German traditions, temperament, language, and religion. While there is nothing very startling or original about these distinctions, it is what Mme. de Staël says after making them that interests us most: "la question pour nous n'est entre la poésie classique et la poésie romantique." She refuses to make a choice. The one type has grown out of a particular civilization, the other out of a different civilization—so different that to compare the epic and the lyric, or find grounds for preference, would seem to be impossible. Only when a nation has imitated, has not allowed its literature to grow from its own soil (France being an example), does the critic find reason to choose or prefer.

One cannot say that eighteenth-century historical interpretations led inevitably to views of this sort. While they have all recognized the close relation of literature and its backgrounds, scholars, historians, readers, and critics have by no means regarded this relation in the same way. The particular historical interpretation is determined by one's purpose or by his prejudices. However, historical criticism, of which Mme. de Staël was an early exponent, has been one of the most important results of emphasis upon literary environment. Rejecting the absolute values of eighteenth-century critics, yet agreeing with them and with Mme. de Staël and Taine that each poem is thoroughly conditioned by time and place, the historical critic has sought to find in history the criteria for evaluating works of art. The nature of a poem is predetermined by the moment of its creation; therefore it must be judged in relation to that moment. It becomes a good or bad expression of one point in history. If it is decided that Jonson's plays had not adequately portrayed life round the beginning of the seventeenth century, those plays are obviously inferior to any plays or poems which had. If it is decided that Homer had really represented the ideas, customs, and beliefs of his time—as nearly all critics before and after Perrault have agreed—then Homer's poetry leaves little to be desired. The historical critic, whatever objections may be raised to his view of literature, has at least offered an escape from the dogmatic and chaotic historical interpretations so common since the eighteenth century.

APPENDIX

The 'Reputation of Blackwell's Enquiry In England

As it was pointed out in Chapter V, a large number of English writers mention Blackwell's book. For example, Mrs. Cockburn informs her niece that the *Enquiry* "has had a great vogue at *London*" and adds that there had been reports "the Queen was pleased with it."[1] Mrs. Cockburn herself was sufficiently well impressed to defend Blackwell from the accusations of a reviewer in the *Republic of Letters*. This reviewer, while professing an unwillingness to attack a work "which has been commended by some whom I would esteem Judges,"[2] says that many readers will find nothing original about the *Enquiry* and others will insist that the subject, manners, language, and religion of Homeric times were "purely adventitious to the Poet."[3] More enthusiastic, on the other hand, were the scholars Sir John Clerk[4] and Roger Gale. Gale speaks of the book as "a most ingenious essay upon Homer & his writings" and further describes it as "the best account of the genius of those early times, & the nature of the poem, that I believe was ever composed."[5] Apparently pleased by the Greek professor's book, even the aging Dr. Bentley did Blackwell "unusual honours" by inviting him to his quarters in Cambridge, where they discussed Homer and Homeric language and orthography at some length.[6]

Bishop Warburton was the first critic of importance to recognize Blackwell's ability as a Homeric scholar. In his often-quoted *Divine Legation of Moses*, he mentions the "learned author" of the *Enquiry*,[7] and cites this work and the *Letters Concerning Mythology* more than once in the course of his rather laborious study.[8] Charles Peters, in answering Warburton, speaks of Blackwell as "a writer of no inconsiderable authority with this gentleman";[9] and he draws some of his own arguments from the Greek professor's works.[10]

1. *The Works of Mrs. Catharine Cockburn, Theological, Moral, Dramatic, and Poetical. Several of Them Now First Printed*, Thomas Birch, ed. (London, 1751), II, 278. Letter dated August 28, 1735. Mrs. Cockburn mentions the book in another letter dated February 20, 1734–35. *Idem*, II, 281.
2. *The Present State of the Republick of Letters*, xv (April, 1735), 293.
3. *Idem*, xv, 308.
4. Clerk had asked Gale to help Blackwell in having the *Enquiry* published.
5. *The Family Memoirs of the Rev. William Stukeley, M.D. and the Antiquarian and Other Correspondence of William Stukeley, Roger and Samuel Gale* (Durham, 1882–87), Publication of the Surtees Society, LXXIII, 276. Letter from R. Gale to Stukeley, August 31, 1734.
6. *Idem*, LXXVI, 27. Letter from Thomas Blackwell to R. Gale, October 2, 1735.
7. Warburton, *The Divine Legation of Moses Demonstrated*, I, 280.
8. *Idem*, II, 334, 340, 341, 342.
9. Charles Peters, *A Critical Dissertation on the Book of Job* (London, 1757), pp. 3–4.
10. *Idem*, pp. 98, 467.

Despite Mrs. Cockburn's report about the book's popularity in London, it seems that few writers even mention the *Enquiry* during the fifteen or twenty years after its first publication. But, with the appearance of a new group of critics, Blackwell's study became increasingly well known. For example, John Gilbert Cooper, the supposed author of *Letters Concerning Taste*, calls Blackwell a "very ingenious and learned Author" and says that he shows how Homer "had personally accompanied his Fancy wherever she roved upon the Face of the Earth."[11] Cooper lists the *Enquiry* after Dubos' *Reflexion critiques sur la poesie* as one of the most important critical works of the time.[12] Joseph Warton, in his *Essay on Pope*, mentions the "excellent" book by Blackwell[13] and says in a footnote that "Blackwell received his just idea of *Homer*, and of the *reasons* and *causes* of *Homer's* superior excellence, from Berkley, with whom he had been connected, and had travelled."[14] In his edition of Virgil's poems, Warton quotes from the *Enquiry* on several occasions, basing many of his observations on the differences between the poetry of Homer and Virgil upon Blackwell's remarks.[15] Twice in the *Observations on the Fairy Queen*, Thomas Warton mentions Blackwell, quoting him at length as an authority on early Greek religion.[16] One wonders how much the *Enquiry* may have influenced Warton, when he says, in speaking of Elizabethan manners and superstitions, that those "who have perused Blackwall's [*sic*] *Enquiry into the Life and Writings of Homer*, will be best qualified to judge how much better enabled that poet is to describe, who copies from living objects, than he who describes, in a later age, from tradition."[17] The passage is particularly interesting, since one of Warton's main contentions was that the manners of the *Fairy Queen* were as real as "the plain descriptions in Homer."[18]

While not agreeing that Homer's superiority can be explained in terms of physical causes,[19] Elizabeth Montagu acknowledges that she was "much delighted" by the *Enquiry*.[20] "It is wrote with fine spirit and imagination, gives one a delightful view of the first ages of the world; shows nature in its simplicity, customs and manners in their infancy, before hypocrisy disguised nature, or luxury corrupted it."[21] In another letter Mrs. Montagu recommends the work to her friend, observing at the same time that Blackwell had been rewarded with "some fame indeed" but with no money

11. John Gilbert Cooper, *Letters Concerning Taste. The Fourth Edition. To Which Are Added, Essays on Similar and Other Subjects* (London, 1771), pp. 20–1.
12. *Idem*, pp. 122–3.
13. J. Warton, *An Essay on the Genius and Writings of Pope*, I, 135.
14. *Idem*, II, 224, n.
15. Pitt and Warton, *The Works of Virgil, in Latin and English*, II, 118–19, n; III, 142–4, 378–9.
16. T. Warton, *Observations on the Fairy Queen of Spenser*, I, 106–07.
17. *Idem*, II, 166.
18. *Idem*, II, 88. Warton again speaks of the *Enquiry*, in a less important connection, in his *History of English Poetry*, III, 400.
19. *The Letters of Mrs. Montagu*, III, 214–15. Letter to Gilbert West, January 6, 1753.
20. *Idem*, I, 262. Letter to the Duchess of Portland, August 2, 1741.
21. *Idem*, I, 263.

from his patron.[22] Since she adopted a historical approach in criticizing Shakespeare, one wonders whether she too may have been affected by Blackwell's treatment of Homer.

Probably no one studied Homer more closely than Edward Gibbon and no one supplemented his studies with a more careful and thorough reading of books which explained the background of the *Iliad* and *Odyssey*. In March, 1762, Gibbon says he had been examining Blackwell's work in order to "get a little nearer to Homer, whom I have never lost sight of";[23] and a month later he was still reading and rereading individual chapters of the book.[24] Gibbon listed the *Enquiry* among the important contributions to Homeric criticism, calling it a "fine though sometimes fanciful effort of genius and learning."[25]

Finally, we shall mention in passing a group of critics who had little to say about the *Enquiry* but who were at least acquainted with the book. In urging modern writers to cease imitating the ancients, Edward Young states that he agrees with Blackwell that the inferiority of present-day poets is due to "some cause far beneath the moon"[26] and not, as some have supposed, to a lack of genius. Richard Hurd employs the testimony of Blackwell in his assertion that later poets imitated Homer in their use of the Greek deities as poetic machinery;[27] and later in the century, in her *Progress of Romance*, Clara Reeve says of Homer, "If we may believe Dr. *Blackwell*, there was a wonderful concurrence of circumstances, that elevated him to this high station; circumstances unlikely, perhaps impossible, to happen again to any other Poet."[28] John Pinkerton mentions the *Enquiry* as one of the three "learned" books of importance to be produced by Scotchmen.[29] Despite the fact that Blackwell had no love for formal criticism, the editor of Aristotle's treatise on poetry speaks of the professor as an "ingenious and entertaining author."[30] Finally, in his long discussion of the origin of Irish poetry, Warner, like John Brown, makes great use of Blackwell's study of Homer and the primitive bards, their occupations and relations to the people.[31]

22. *Idem*. i, 296. Letter to the Duchess of Portland, October 11, 1741.

23. *Gibbon's Journal to January 28th, 1763. My Journal I, II, & III and Ephemerides,* D. M. Low, ed. (London, 1929), p. 49. Entry for March 18, 1762.

24. *Idem*, p. 57. Entry for April 14, 1762.

25. MS. note in *The Miscellaneous Works of Edward Gibbon, Esq. with Memoirs of His Life and Writings, Composed by Himself: Illustrated from His Letters,* John, Lord Sheffield, ed. (London, 1814), v, 582.

26. *Edward Young's Conjectures on Original Composition,* E. J. Morley, ed. (Manchester, 1918), p. 10.

27. "On Poetical Imitation," in *Q. Horatii Flacci Epistolae,* ii, 163.

28. Reeve, *The Progress of Romance,* i, 19.

29. John Pinkerton, *An Enquiry into the History of Scotland Preceding the Reign of Malcolm III. or the Year 1056. Including the Authentic History of That Period* (London, 1794), i, xi.

30. Thomas Twining, *Aristotle's Treatise of Poetry Translated: with Notes on the Translation, and on the Original; and Two Dissertations, on Poetical, and Musical Imitation* (London, 1812), i, 65, n.

31. Ferdinando Warner, *The History of Ireland* (London, 1763), i, 57, 63–4, 117.

INDEX*

* Homer has not been included because the name appears on nearly every page.

A